Third Eye

Mind Power, Intuition and Psychic Awareness

3rd Edition

By Alex McKenna

Contents

Introduction

Chapter 1: What Is The Third Eye?

Chapter 2: Why Should You Activate The Third Eye?

Chapter 3: Third Eye Meditation

Chapter 4: Imagination: Front And Centered

Chapter 5: How To Open Your Third Eye

Chapter 6: Experiences After The Opening Of The Third Eye

Chapter 7: FAQ's About The Third Eye

Chapter 8 – Things You Should Know

Chapter 9 - Healing Your Third Eye

Chapter 10 - Feeding your Chakra for Increased Intuition

Chapter 11 - Some Facts About The Third Eye

Chapter 12 – Common Problems Faced

Chapter 13 - 7 Steps To Increase Your Clairvoyant Power

Chapter 14 - Activating the Third Eye through Body Purification

Chapter 15 - Why Should You Activate Your Third Eye?

Chapter 16: Unconventional Ways of Opening the Third Eye

Chapter 17: Mistakes to Avoid When Trying To Increase Your Intuition

Chapter 18: Experiences upon Opening Your Third Eye

Chapter 19: Things You Should Know About Your 'Third Eye'

Chapter 20: How To Tell If You Are Having A Spiritual Or A Psychic Awakening

Chapter 21: Mediums and Intuition

BONUS CHAPTER - Three Secret Tips for Opening Your Third Eye

Conclusion

i

Introduction

If we were to know the true meaning of life, why we were born and other such questions could be answered, how much simpler would it be? If we could see beyond the past and present to the future, how many struggles could we overcome?

Each person comes into the world with some purpose and they hardly realize it till they reach the end of it. Everyone is busy in just trying to get through each day and make a brighter future. But no one really knows what that future actually holds and when it will arrive.

People try to find the answers to such questions in different manners. Some could just think over it in a practical way and try to plan out their actions for a better result. However there are others who chose a more unconventional route. At some point or the other, people are always intrigued by the potential of the mystical.

If you have chosen this book, you are one of the latter. However, it does not necessarily have to be completely isolated from the first either. This is what is proved by the concept of the third eye.

You will be reading about what the third eye is all about. There are many associations to science as well as culture when it comes to this topic. Quite a few people turn to seers and other such people who claim to see beyond the obvious and even into the future. With this book, you will gain a better understanding of the realities of such things and how it happens. While some such people might be carrying out scams, some have awakened or activated the third eye. This is what gives them a deeper knowledge of what is within as well as beyond what we can see.

As you go through all the information in this book, you will also learn how you can persevere to open your third eye. This will help you in different aspects and make you conscious on a much higher level than others who are ignorant of such knowledge.

Chapter 1: What Is The Third Eye?

The third eye also called the inner eye is an esoteric and mystical concept referring to an invisible eye, which offers perception beyond the ordinary sight. In some spiritual traditions such as in Hinduism, the third eye refers to the chakra, brow or ajna. In Theosophy, the third eye is related to the pineal gland. The third eye is considered as the gate that leads to the inner realms or higher level of consciousness.

In New Age spirituality, the third eye is often symbolized as a state of enlightenment or the ability to evoke mental images that have deeply psychological significance. It is often associated with out of body experiences, religious visions, ability to observe auras and chakras, clairvoyance and precognition. Sometimes people who claim to have the ability to see through their third eye are known as seers.

In many traditional beliefs like Hinduism, the third eye is believed to be located in the center of the forehead, a little above the eyebrow junction. Other traditions such as Theosophy believe the third eye is connected with the pineal gland. As per this theory, human beings during prehistoric times actually had a third eye at the back of their head with a spiritual and physical function. With time, as human beings evolved, this eye shrunk and sunk into what is known today as the pineal gland. As per the hypothesis by Dr. Rick Strassman, the pineal gland, which is lightly sensitive, produces and releases dimethyltryptamine (DMT); an entheogen that he believes could possibly be excreted in large quantities during moments of birth or death.

In many Chinese religious sects and Taoism, the training of the third eye requires focusing attention on the area between the eyebrows with closed eyes, while the body lies in a variety of qigong postures. The goal of the training is to allow the body to tune into the perfect vibration of the universe and to gain solid foundation required to reach advanced levels of meditation. Taoism also teaches that the third eye is located between the two physical eyes, and reaches up to the middle of the forehead when opened fully. It teaches that the third eye located at the sixth chakra forms part of the main meridian, the line that separates the right and left hemispheres of the body, and is one of the most important energy centers of the body.

The third eye, or the inner eye as it is sometimes known, refers to a person's ability to see beyond what is visible to the normal eye. The concept refers to the invisible eye that each person has with which they can perceive inner realms and spaces of higher consciousness.

The third eye symbolizes a means of attaining deep consciousness and even enlightenment at a higher level. As you give more importance to the significance of the third eye and work towards it's awakening, you will see what it really means. People who are able to activate their third eye are the ones who have had visions, out of body experiences and experienced such phenomenon, which might seem otherworldly. The truth is that the third eye is the gateway through which they are actually able to view their inner self as well as the entire world outside on a greater scale with deeper understanding.

The Third Eye is an entryway to a space of consciousness of the inner worlds. Through it, the body of energy within is awakened and governed. In simple terms, the third eye can be described as a trigger, which activates higher frequencies of the body of energy consequently leading to higher conscious states. In even simpler terms, the third eye provides perception beyond ordinary sight.

As the gate to the deeper realms of higher consciousness, the Third Eye symbolizes enlightenment. Hinduism describes it as the Ajna or brow Chakra. While in theosophy, it is closely related to the pineal gland. Those who have opened, and can use the Third Eye are called seers. Seers can experience religious visions, clairvoyance, observe chakras and auras as well as have precognition and out-of-body experiences.

The Third Eye is positioned at the center of the forehead slightly above the junction of the eyebrows. Early human generations are believed to have had an eye in the back of their heads. This eye had both physical and spiritual functions but as evolution took its course, the eye became more and more vestigial. Eventually, it atrophied and sunk into the present-day anatomical pineal gland.

As such the Third Eye:

> Is the seat of the soul?
> A telepathic power point

➤ A gateway to inner worlds and realms of higher consciousness
➤ A connection to divine guidance
➤ A portal to another existence.

Both eastern as well as western culture has philosophies in relation to the third eye. Although the details of it may differ in some, the essence of it is the same.

Cultural association

As informed earlier, in Hinduism, the third eye is associated with the Ajna chakra. It is said to be the center of intuition and wisdom. It is the 6th chakra and is positioned behind the middle of the forehead. The chakra is associated with purple color and has various images depicting it.

A seed mantra of the sound "Aum" is associated with this chakra. This chakra has special significance according to Hindu tradition as it is considered a gateway for spiritual energy. The energy that goes in through here can also be bad so they take care to try and protect it from harmful external forces. This is why they have traditional practices of drawing symbols on the forehead with materials like vermillion.

In order to attain enlightenment, it is essential to meditate with this chakra in focus. This will allow the person to connect with the supreme powers or God. When a person works to balance all the chakras in the body, each individual chakra needs to be taken into account. If the third eye chakra is in balance, the person has better intuition, focus, thinking and generally good health.

In Buddhism, the third eye is a common symbol in artworks related to religion. It is a focal point of meditation in their culture as well. They call it the eye of consciousness, which can allow them to see beyond the physical world around them. The statue of the Lord Buddha has a dot at the center of the forehead depicting this third eye. The third eye symbolizes the awakening of higher consciousness and true wisdom. Dedicated meditation with this chakra is considered crucial for the person to attain enlightenment.

Pineal Gland

A small endocrine gland known as the Pineal gland is present near the center of the brain. It is thus named due to the pinecone like shape of the gland and is also known as the third eye. It is situated near the center between the two halves of the brain. A hormone known as melatonin is produced here.

Keeping aside the physiological science of this gland, it has always been associated to the concept of the third eye. The gland is said to be a link between the physical world and the spiritual realms. It also works in harmonizing various functions in the body. Many spiritual philosophies from around the world relate the pineal gland as the third eye and associate it with clairvoyance and enlightenment.

Third eye for Seers

Going to the topic of seers you will also realize how much it has to do with the third eye. Harnessing the ability of the third eye is how such people are able to display abilities, which might seem like magic to some. Opening of the third eye results in increased intuition, beyond what a normal person can experience. Intuition can work as a gut feeling or a kind of vision.

When your third eye is awoken, your mind combines all the information and is able to predict or guide towards an outcome. Using this intuition and other techniques together helps seers in their art.

Patterning is an ancient practice seen as a part of Taoism originally. While some see it as a simple practice, it involves more complexities. Intuition is used to see the possibilities in something. The third eye then helps to visualize the potential of it on a deeper level and make out the pattern related to it.

You can use patterning with regard to every aspect in life. As your third eye is activated, you are more open or receptive to everything in the world. This helps in patterning and predicting how you can act in order to move your life in a positive direction. Seers use patterning to display their skills to others although it might appear as simple divination.

As you learn more about the third eye and patterning you get better at it. The more you work on the activation of the third eye, the more you can nurture its potentials as well. This opens you up to all the potential of an opened third eye. All this knowledge and greater understanding is coupled with the deeper connection with the universe. This helps with understanding the potential of the life you take into account. People who are unaware of such things think that it is all about people who can predict the future or fortune of a person. A genuine person, who studies patterning and is in touch with the higher consciousness with their third eye, knows differently. They use their intuition and patterning in order to understand how a certain person's life might unfold as a consequence of their actions. This is how "predictions" actually work.

Once you start meditating and stimulate your third eye, it becomes a much easier concept to grasp. It will give you better insight into both your life and those around you.

Third Eye Chakra (Ajna)

The Third Eye chakra is not directly connected to the concept of the Third Eye, though it shares similar aspects. The seven chakras are considered to be energy centers that help maintain body function and mental and spiritual awareness. Each chakra can be opened, developed, and has particular attributes associated with it to stimulate and help maintain its health.

The Third Eye chakra is numbered six and is located at the center of the forehead between the eyebrows. Its function can be simplified as our ability to focus on and see the big picture. It is connected with intuition, imagination, wisdom, the ability to think and make decisions, and clairvoyance. Indigo is its associated color with "OM" as it's associated sound, so focusing on these is thought to help stimulate it. The hypothalamus, pituitary gland, and autonomic nervous system (controlling breathing, heart rate, etc.) are all attributed to the Third Eye chakra.

Chapter 2: Why Should You Activate The Third Eye?

Everyone knows and is aware of the two eyes each person has. However in reality each person has three has. While the two eyes that we actively use for vision are extremely important, the third eye has immense significance. This is the eye that helps you see beyond what is right in front of you and further into things you did not even know existed.

To some people the concept of the third eye may seem like non-sense and myths. Some traditions even consider it as a link to evil. However in others it is considered a means towards higher levels of intellect and consciousness. The levels to which people believe in the strength of the third eye may vary. Certain traditions believe that it is the gateway to enlightenment and a path to connect with their God. Others just believe in the basic essence of how this third eye chakra can increase their awareness of life to a higher level and understand the true meaning or significance of everything.

The purpose of harnessing the power of the third eye is to try and get a better understanding of yourself and life. It also helps you to truly discover who you are and what you can do. Many people just shy away from such thoughts and go through their entire life at a monotonous pace, without any meaning. However, the third eye can make an immense difference.

- You can see beyond what is physically in front of you and visible through normal eyesight.
- You have a sense of things that your other five senses cannot perceive.
- You get a sense of the people who are not physically present with you.
- You can hear beyond the sounds around you. Inner voices as well as sounds from other frequencies will be more audible.
- Your actions will change in a positive way.
- You will gain better understanding.
- Your beliefs will change and get founded.
- You become more receptive to the energies around you. This is how clairvoyants are able to see visions, auras, non-physical beings, etc. Since their third eye is more receptive than those with a blocked eye, they have greater ability to see beyond normal vision.
- You decrease the limitations set on you and become more open to things.
- Your intuition increases.
- Any skills and talents that a person has are enhanced.
- Your perception of a situation will change. Any situation, which comes before, you or one, which has already happened, will appear to you in a new light. Prejudice or any negative notions do not block your mind. This helps you react better.

- You become more connected with the universe. You also connect better with the spiritual guides.
- Your ability to learn and remember things also increases. Your understanding will go even beyond analysis and reasoning.
- You start becoming more aware of what happened in the past.
- It helps you deal with issues that have always troubled you and hindered your peace of mind.
- Astral travel becomes a possibility for you as your third eye gets activated.
- Life becomes more meaningful and peaceful at the same time.

The third eye is a vital field of energy and tapping into it helps you to receive more from outward as well as within. It works as a sixth sense which is capable of being aware of much more than what the other five senses can take in. For instance, if a person has no sight or hearing, it is considered a disability. The same way, when the third eye is closed, you cannot sense its purpose. It has a unique capability to link you with higher energies that you are otherwise blind towards.

As you persevere to open your third eye, you will be more intuitive. It will help you understand the true meaning of life and your purpose. You can easily deal with what comes your way and answer your own questions. As your third eye opens, the truth seems to unfold by itself. Problems that you previously stressed over will become simple and insignificant. You then realize how much energy you spent and get anxious over unnecessary things. Your ability to handle stress or any emotions increases. It helps you gain more control over your mind and actions.

Meditation with the third eye helps you look into yourself and get a clear understanding of your inner self. If you were previously unsure about anything or could not decide on things, it gets much easier as you release your mind to this state.

Chapter 3: Third Eye Meditation

During the days following the first opening, do lots of meditation and keep repeating the technique until you perfect it. The initial meditation stages introduce the meditator to transcendence states while systematically building the Third eye. They also train the mind to be truly silent by helping you build a structure beyond your thoughts where the mind can be mastered and made silent.

Preparations

- ✓ Take off your shoes, ties, belt or any other form of restrictive clothing or jewelry
- ✓ Sit on the floor or chair, back straight and legs crossed; this allows energy to flow freely through you

Phase 1

- ➤ Close your eyes, keep them shut throughout your meditation
- ➤ Breathe creating a friction in your throat such that a vibration develops within the larynx
- ➤ Adjust your spine; ensure your back is upright, and the neck, head, and back are all in a straight line

➤ Cultivate absolute stillness and tranquility

Phase 2

➤ Begin to become aware of the vibration in between the eyebrows
➤ Connect this vibration with the vibration in the throat i.e. become aware of the two vibrations at the same time
➤ The throat vibration acts as an amplifier that cultivates and builds the vibration in between the eyebrows.

Phase 3

➤ Drop your awareness of the vibration in the throat and begin to look for a fog, haze, color, glow or light forming between the eyebrows.
➤ These manifestations are more spiritual than physical. It is thus vital for the meditator not to imagine or visualize false manifestations.
➤ Use your throat vibration to connect to any slight manifestation that you perceive. Try to amplify this using throat vibration
➤ As the manifestation becomes more pronounced, gradually drop your awareness of the throat vibration.
➤ Focus on the brighter or vivid aspects of the manifestation and ignore the hazier aspects

Phase 4

➤ Begin to focus on the background of the manifestation. This will give you a feeling of a space opening up and extending in front of you.
➤ You can now drop the throat vibration as you allow yourself to be absorbed by this space

Phase 5

> ➤ Allow yourself to spiral forwards and clockwise such that you fall and spin into the space tunnel
> ➤ Let yourself be caught up in the vortex of the space
> ➤ As you fall, the qualities of the space will change, and you will be projected into an entirely different reality

Phase 6: The Non-Technique

> ➤ Drop the awareness of everything else and focus above the head
> ➤ Lose everything else including yourself; do nothing else apart from being aware
> ➤ Be motionless, lose complete control and let the awareness take over

Finishing the Meditation

> ➤ Begin to listen to the sounds outside
> ➤ Become aware of your body
> ➤ Inhale deeply several times and then slowly drift into full consciousness.

Meditation helps you to relax your mind and body but increase your ability to focus on something. In order to open or activate your third eye, meditation plays a crucial role. There are different types of meditation and it may work differently from person to person. However, it is essential to go through the practice on a regular basis in order to achieve the state of awareness of the third eye.

> ➤ First find an appropriate space to meditate. It should be a separate area, which has no distractions and will allow you to focus on your meditation at the maximal level. The space doesn't have to be completely silent and soundproof. It can be a quiet room in the house or outside in a park. But a room where the television

is on or a road where cars are honking will obviously not be ideal. Once you find your space, make sure no one disturbs you for the duration of your meditation.

➢ Do some warm up exercises, which will loosen the tense muscles in your body and also make your mind more alert.

➢ Now find the posture in which you can meditate the best. One of the best and common postures is the lotus or half lotus position. Sitting with your legs crossed and keeping your hands over your knees will be quite comfortable. Make sure to keep your back erect and stay alert. Close your eyes but don't get sleepy. Staying alert does not mean being tense. You need to relax both your mind and body as you begin meditation.

➢ Once you feel your body is relaxed, work on your mind. Clear your head from all thoughts and let it relax. Draw your attention towards what is happening around you or even within. Listen to the subtle sounds near you and focus on your breathing. Notice how your breath goes in and out as you push away thoughts of anything else. Clearing your mind from such thoughts takes time and patience. The first half of each meditative session comprises of this time to clear your mind. Only then can you go further.

➢ You should stay calm yet determined throughout your meditation. Firstly, it requires daily practice to learn the proper way to meditate. Giving up on it will be fruitless. The results are not instant but they are more than worth it. Each time you sit to meditate, your mind might often lose focus. Don't let this irritate you or make you give up. Just stay firm and divert your mind back to the task at hand. Concentrating on breathing is especially useful in blocking out distractions.

➢ As you start blocking out all thoughts, focus on the position of the third eye. Move your attention to the center of your forehead, between your eyebrows where the third eye is supposed to be. As you focus there, you will see a point of light appear. Keep your attention on that emitted light. Visualize this light spreading in all directions from that source.

➢ Don't think of anything while you concentrate on this. There should be no fear or uncertainty about it. Keep breathing and concentrate on the light from the chakra.

➢ As you focus on the light, let the source get brighter and brighter. It should send more and more light out as you do this.

➢ As you get better at this, your body and mind will be completely relaxed. This allows your third eye to open further. Open yourself to the higher forces and let the guide you further.

➢ As you connect with your higher state of consciousness and the forces to act on you, allow the light to fill your entire body and soul.

➢ At this point there might be certain thoughts or questions that arise. Allow them to unfold on their own. You will receive energy from around you.

➢ As you feel the experience start to wane, allow yourself to come back to the present. Don't push yourself too fast. Allow it to happen slowly and bring you back to the present.

➢ Take deep breaths and start becoming aware of your body and the things around you.

Chanting meditation:

➢ You should start the same way as before and continue your breathing exercises. Once you have set aside all distractions and can focus solely on your breathing, move on to the next step.

➢ Now perform the shambhavi mudra. You need to turn your eyes upwards towards the center of the forehead at the third eye chakra. Look at it but don't strain your eyes while doing this. Just try to get your eyes in this position in a relaxed manner.

➢ Now take a deep breath in through your nose and keep your mouth closed. Hold the tip of your tongue between your teeth and gently bite down on it.

➢ Take your breath out through the mouth. Chant the word "thoh" as you do this. This sends vibrations to the third eye. The "th" sound should resonate as you do this and focus on opening your third eye.

➢ The tone of vibration should be correct. It is usually in the "a", "b" or "c" tone. You will feel the vibration when you try them out.

➢ Don't rush through the process. Do the breathing and chanting in a slow and steady manner. As you exhale slowly, your lungs are ready to take in the air from your next deep breath in.

➢ Notice how you feel the vibration at the center of your forehead. Your thoughts should all be directed in a positive direction. Think thoughts of love and compassion, which send positive energy.

➢ As you exhale, take another deep breath. Then exhale and chant again. Keep repeating this at least 5 times. Continue the exercise regularly for a few days. This will help you gain more focus and get a head start on third eye meditation. As you finish this exercise you will start noticing a slight pressure at the area of your third eye.

➢ After completing this for about 5 days move on to the next step.

➢ Assume an erect posture in the lotus position again.

➢ Do the regular breathing exercises. Take a deep breath in through your nose and take it out slowly through your mouth. Think of all the negativity inside you as you exhale and imagine it all coming out with your breath. It should give you a cleansing feeling from all stress and frustration.

➢ Repeat the shambhavi mudra again and focus on the third eye.

➢ Visualize a purple color at the third eye and feel how bright and positive it is.

➢ Chant in a c tone and notice the vibrations reverberate at your chakra. This will keep your opened chakra stimulated.

➢ As you focus on the third eye think of all the positive things you want in life. Don't try to force an image of something that you want. Let the picture unfold by itself as you realize what is really important to you and will give you true happiness. Your higher consciousness will help you realize this.

> Practice this every day after the first few days of opening your chakra. Your third eye needs constant stimulation in order to stay active and balanced. As you build a strong foundation for the working of the chakra, you will see how you become more receptive to higher things.

You need to realize that opening the third eye takes a lot of time and determination. A high level of discipline is required to be able to achieve that state of consciousness. Expecting the results to appear fast will be pointless. However, it is also said that people who had more experience with this and were spiritually more awakened in previous lives, will be able to open their third eye faster in this life as well. The time will vary from person to person based on various factors. People spend years trying to even meditate properly without allowing any distractions. Opening the third eye will need you to get rid of all such blockages so that you let the higher forces act on you.

Chapter 4: Imagination: Front And Centered

What is this "Third Eye" more and more of us are learning about? We have seen many references to it throughout history, perhaps without even knowing it. A small dot between the eyebrows in Hindu and Buddhist cultures points to it, it's on the back of the dollar bill in a pyramid, and we've heard many references to it as "the mind's eye," "the all-seeing eye," "the eye of enlightenment," and so on. So does it actually exist, and if so, what can it do for us? Let's take a step into the slightly unknown and shed some light on it.

Where does it come from?

The largest understanding of this somewhat esoteric concept derives from two viewpoints that share similar attributes and correlations. The first is found in Theosophy, which maintains that knowledge of God can be reached through spiritual ecstasy (enlightenment), made popular by Helena Blavatsky's, The Secret Doctrine, published in 1888.

Theosophy regards the 3rd eye to be associated with the pineal gland. In *The Secret Doctrine,* Blavatsky claims that the third eye is no longer active in people, which used to be located at the back of the head long ago but has sunk into the middle of the head since, leaving the pineal gland behind as the only remnant. She does acknowledge that it can be activated and developed, but did not recommend it in her time.

Hinduism, another viewpoint that makes mention of the Third Eye, first recorded its existence in the Vedas (1700 BCE – 1100 BCE) as the Third Eye chakra, also known as the "Ajna" or "brow chakra". The Hindus believe the Third Eye chakra or "eye of knowledge" to be a channel to inner power. The Third Eye chakra is closely associated with the pituitary gland, which helps regulate all hormonal activity in the body. Buddhism, sharing the depiction of the Hindu Third Eye as a dot between the brows, regards this as the symbol of spiritual awakening of knowledge and wisdom. Taoism also sees the Third Eye as a symbol of profound awareness.

The correlations of these concepts from both Theosophy and Hinduism among others has led to further theories on the depiction of the Third Eye in other ancient cultures.

The Ancient Egyptians depict the eye of Horus - a sky god, son of Ra, the sun god – in many hieroglyphs. It is believed that this eye is symbolic for the thalamic cortex in the center of the brain, specifically representing the thalamus, hypothalamus and pituitary gland. Some have found this glyph's parts to be directly proportionate to its entirety as well, mirroring the golden ratio of Fibonacci's famous spiral.

Since the pineal gland derives its name from the "pine" nut, many others have attributed the pinecone to its symbolic representation.

Pinecones

Indeed, the pinecone has its roots in many ancient artifacts as a symbol for consciousness and enlightenment.

The staff of Osiris in Egypt, dated to approximately 1224 B.C., is depicted as a scepter entwined by two snakes spiraling up its length to a pinecone placed at the top. Scholars have associated the snakes of this staff to the same depiction of snakes rising up the spine in the Hindu practice of Kundalini, which is said to lead to enlightenment. We see a replica of this symbol on ambulances today to represent health.

In Greek and Roman mythology the god Dionysus or Bacchus, respectively, was often shown with a staff made of fennel and topped with a pinecone. Sitting in front of the Roman Catholic Vatican today is an enormous bronze sculpture of a pinecone known as the "Pigna". Its origins have been traced back to Ancient Rome in which it was used as a water fountain next to the Temple of Isis, the Egyptian goddess.

Assyrian palace carvings from 713 – 716 B.C. expose four-winged deities intentionally holding pinecones the same way we see the bald eagle of the United States clutching 13 arrows in one talon to represent the original 13 colonies and an olive branch in the other, symbolizing peace.

Pinecones are regarded for their embodiment of sacred geometry, that is, the perfect mathematical structure seen in organic growth such as conch and snail shells, sunflowers and roses, as well as inorganic materials like crystals. These organisms reflect the golden ratio, which in application results with a pattern in the parts of the whole, staying true as the whole grows larger. Names like Plato, Euclid, and

Fibonacci are famous in mathematics as contributors to the golden ratio theorem.

The pattern observed in pinecones is that their scales spiral around the cone's center, which can be traced perfectly in both clockwise and counter-clockwise directions. This exemplifies Fibonacci's spiral, based on the mathematical value of phi and the golden ratio, which is widely regarded in sacred geometry.

Sacred geometry

The basic principle of sacred geometry is the ability to replicate perfect structures in both increasing and decreasing quantities by employing the same pattern. Imagine drawing an equilateral triangle, then drawing another equilateral triangle, upside-down, inside of that one. The points of the smaller triangle will automatically touch the midpoints on the sides of the larger one. Instantly you have created three more triangles inside the larger one, which are the same size as the smaller triangle. You can even go further to draw triangles inside the smaller ones and so on.

Focusing on this principle allows us to direct our focus from microscopic components to macroscopic ones and back again. We can see how the structure and nature of atoms reflect those of our solar system.

Adolf Zeising, mathematician and philosopher of the mid 1800s, found the golden ratio expressed in the human body among many other things. He found patterns in the correspondence of facial features and other proportions like the size of a person's foot being in equal length to the size of their forearm. Zeising believed this geometric principle is spread as a spiritual ideal through both nature and art in all forms on the grand scale of our universe. He also suggests that it finds its fullest realization in the human form. As a tribute to his studies, several other researchers in recent years have implicated human DNA to reflect the golden ratio.

Recognizing the patterns of sacred geometry around and within us helps bring understanding to the nature of our universe. As we reach a deeper awareness of our external environment and internal environment like that of our bodies, we tune in to utilizing our Third Eye function.

Thalamic Cortex

The thalamic cortex is located in the center of the brain. It contains some of the most important components for maintaining regularity of brain and bodily function, including emotions.

The corpus callosum sits like a roof at the top of the thalamus cortex and acts as a communications bridge between the two hemispheres of the brain. Below that is the thalamus, which relays signals for motor and sensory functions like breathing, heart rhythm, muscular movement, pain, touch, smell, sight, and so on, all of which have an intrinsic tie to our sense of awareness.

The hypothalamus is considered the "master gland" that governs all hormonal activity in the body. It stimulates physical growth, monitors serotonin ("happy" hormone) and cortisol ("stress" hormone) levels, and tells the pituitary gland what to do. Tightly working together, the hypothalamus and pituitary gland regulate all processes having to do with stress, rage, fear, body temperature, thirst, hunger, sexual activity, and survival in general.

The pineal gland is located in a tiny fold behind and above the pituitary gland with the brain stem between them. This gland used to be considered functionless by the medical community for many years, aligning with the claims of Blavatsky, however now it is medically understood to produce three hormones – serotonin, melatonin, and DMT.

Serotonin is directly linked to our emotions, the production and reception of which increases our sense of joy and blissfulness. It has been noted conversely that the lack of serotonin production or reception in the brain is a leading cause of clinical depression. So then, we may see how this pineal gland and its activation may be associated in the "blissful states" that are claimed to be achieved in enlightenment.

Melatonin is the hormone that invokes us to sleep. The pineal gland is triggered to produce melatonin by total darkness and is triggered to cease production in the presence of light. Scientists have discovered that it doesn't matter if light is shining on the eyelids to stimulate the body to wake up. Light can shine on any part of the body, chest, leg or otherwise, to slow melatonin production. In the world today with nightlights, streetlights and electronic devices shining through all hours of the night, insufficient melatonin production has become an issue. A lack of melatonin leads to difficulty falling or staying asleep, which involves a system that can create quite adverse effects on one's health.

There are five stages of sleep that incur different brainwave activity and body function. When we are awake and dealing with tasks, to-do lists and responsibilities, we are most often operating in beta waves that move very fast. The times just before falling asleep and just after waking up are when we are in Stage I of sleep between beta and slower alpha waves, during which it is easiest to recall our dreams. While the exact purpose of dreaming remains unknown, some psychologists propose it to be grounds for us to problem solve and act out suppressed emotions in symbolic form, thereby releasing the stress caused by the more taxing emotions. We can also consider that many innovators have realized their inventions by waking up from a dream and writing down the ideas derived from it.

Stage II is predominantly theta wave mode. When we can achieve this level through meditation, our mind's grip on task organization loosens and we are able to clarify solutions more easily. Stage III is a deep-sleep pattern known as delta waves, intermixed with slightly faster brain waves. Stage IV is when only delta waves are emitted from the brain. This is the deepest form of sleep, during which hormones from the hypothalamus and pituitary glands are secreted that enable new growth in children and adolescents' bodies, and repair and regeneration for adults. REM (rapid eye movement) sleep is the stage in which dreams occur and heart rate and blood pressure approach waking levels.

The kicker is that because of stress, a fast-paced lifestyle, insomnia, and other factors that prevent a good night's sleep, oftentimes people are not able to reach Stage IV, so their bodies and minds become burdened from not getting the necessary time to repair and regenerate. This can lead to a cycle that increases a prominence of stress in our life, preventing us from thinking clearly and being the best that we can be. When we are stressed we are less likely to be able to cope with life's challenges. When we're relaxed our thoughts flow much more succinctly, allowing us to be more flexible, creative, and effectively productive

Chapter 5: How To Open Your Third Eye

Activating and Maintaining the Third Eye function

Specific mudras, or chants in the Hindu and Ayurvedic philosophies, are said to help activate and maintain the health of each chakra. For the Third Eye chakra it is recommended to chant "OM" in a quiet place for 1 – 20 minutes. There are also musical compositions that are designed to resonate with each specific chakra based on their individual tonal frequency. The frequencies for the Third Eye chakra are noted at 144 Hz, 288 Hz and 576 Hz.

Meditation is by far the most widely used practice for tapping into the Third Eye. While there are numerous forms of meditation, the basic idea is to slow down the thought process. How many times have we had the word for something on the tip of our tongue yet the more we try to think of what it is, the harder it is to recall? And later we find that when we have taken our minds off of it, the word comes to us easily and instantly!

This is why sleep stages and brain waves are inclusive, because many successful practitioners of meditation have described its purpose as bringing cognitive awareness to deeper levels of brain function where theta and delta waves are distinct. It is here where we are proposed to develop control over stress reduction and the healing processes of our bodies as seen naturally occurring in Stage IV sleep.

Dr. Nipun Aggarwal, MD, MBA, MHT, and José Silva are two notable authorities who have developed approaches to "mind control," training our mind's eye to consciously, effectively, and almost immediately regulate bodily functions for optimal health. These approaches are also geared toward maintaining focus and peace of mind in challenging and stressful, everyday situations, memorizing and quickly recalling vast amounts of information, as well as fluent problem solving beyond our five senses.

Using the third eye does not mean developing magical powers or becoming a psychic. It actually implies controlling your mind more effectively and enjoying a deeper sense of intuition to your surroundings. Unfortunately, this shift does not happen overnight, you will need to dedicate your life to spiritual practices that involves practicing awareness of the mind every day.

The First Opening

Choose a day when you have lots of free time ahead of you, for instance at the start of a weekend. This lets you focus intimately on the eye-opening practices. Usually, it gets easier after the first opening. You can do it with friends or alone. It is preferable if you wear light-colored clothes. The first opening isn't very intense; you might just feel a tingling between the eyebrows.

Technique

- ✓ Go to a quiet, tranquil place where you are sure not to be bothered for at least an hour.
- ✓ Light candles around the place
- ✓ Remove your shoes, watch, tie, belt and any other restrictive clothing or jewelry
- ✓ Lie down on the floor, carpet, blanket or mat with your arms on your sides and palms facing up
- ✓ Close your eyes, relax for about 3 minutes and them hum for 5 to 10 minutes

Phase 1

- ➤ Begin breathing through the throat gradually becoming aware of the vibration within the larynx
- ➤ Continue breathing for 5 to 10 minutes and in case your body or consciousness moves, let it be

Phase 2

- ➤ While maintaining the friction in the throat, shift your awareness to the region between your eyebrows
- ➤ It is important that you flow with your body's energy. Do not pay attention to time

Phase 3

- ➤ Place your palm on the area between the eyebrows about 3 to 5 centimeters away from the skin

Phase 4

- ➤ You can have the hand in phase 3 position or by your side
- ➤ With the eyes closed and larynx vibrating, begin to look for a vibration or tingling between the eyebrows.
- ➤ You may also feel a blurry pressure, density or weight
- ➤ Do not focus too hard, just remain vacant and let things take their own course

Phase 5

> ➤ As soon as you feel a vibration or something between your eyebrows try to connect it to the friction in your throat.
> ➤ The vibration will gradually become subtle yet more intense at the same time.
> ➤ Some people may feel the vibration in other parts of the body or on the entire forehead. This is normal; just focus on the vibration between the eyebrows.

Phase 6

> ➤ Stop the vibration in the Larynx
> ➤ Focus on the vibration between the eyebrows
> ➤ Be very still and try to focus on the energy around you
> ➤ Be aware of any light or colors between the eyebrows

Remember

> ✓ Keep your eyes closed throughout the process
> ✓ Do not grasp or focus too much on the region between the eyebrows as this might block the process
> ✓ If you are practicing with friends, do not touch each other
> ✓ If the experience overwhelms you, open your eyes to come back to normal consciousness

For the first experience, the manifestations of the eye are not as important as getting the technique right. Minor bodily movements such as twitching as well as flashing in and out of consciousness may also occur during the first opening. Ignore them and perfect your technique as if nothing happened.

Learning How To Meditate

To begin with, you will need to find the right environment. Choose a place where you can be left alone for at least 30 to

45 min and is relatively quiet. It doesn't need to be completely silent, but try finding a place where you will not be distracted a lot.

Start By Getting Into A Meditative Posture

Sitting on the ground with crossed legs, straight back and hands resting on the knees is considered to be a very effective meditative posture. If you're unable to sit on the ground, sit on a chair and keep your back straight. Support your upper body using your abdominal muscles, and do not allow your back to slouch over. Keep your shoulders down and point your chest out.

Relax Your Body

All of us hold tensions in our body while going through our daily life, which makes focusing very difficult. You will not realize how tensed your muscles are until you consciously try to relax them. Roll your head from side to side to loosen up your body, allow your neck muscles to release and your shoulders to drop.

Relax Your Mind

This is one of the most essential parts of opening the third eye. Perhaps, it is also the most challenging one because you will need to remove all thoughts from your head. You can do this by focusing your attention on any one aspect of the physical world, whether it's the sensation of the ground under you, sound of traffic moving past or your breath going in and out.

While it's nearly impossible to eliminate all thoughts, if a thought does come into your mind, just acknowledge it and allow it to disappear from your mind. You will need a lot of patience and practice to clear your thoughts effectively.

People generally find it very difficult to meditate during the first 10 to 20 min. Give yourself some time to transition from the world outside to a meditative state.

Develop A Habit Of Meditating

The more you think about meditating, the better you'll get at it. You can think about meditation while eating your food, going for a walk or even while brushing your teeth. Even by meditating for just 5 min a day, you will train yourself to become more aware mindfully over time. Use a timer while meditating, as it will stop you from wondering how much time you've already spent meditating.

Open The Intuitive Part Of The Brain

Begin by observing the world around you. People who are generally shy tend to be more intuitive than the average person simply because they spend a lot of time observing other people; and by doing so they develop a higher understanding of things like facial expression, body language and other types of non-explicit communication. These people are very good at detecting sexual chemistry, lies, hidden messages and sarcasm.

You can practice intuition by going to a public place like a cafe, restaurant or park on your own and simply observe other people around you. Try to listen into their conversation without being overbearing or rude. Try to create a story in your mind on how these people got together or about what they are talking about or any other information that you find interesting. The more you will do this, the better you'll get at it.

You can also practice it while sitting around the table with your friends or family, try being quiet for some time and just listen to what they are talking about. Observe people who are not participating in the conversation and watch their reaction to the ongoing interaction. Try and imagine what they might be thinking about when they are not talking. The more you practice it, the better you'll get at.

Dreams Are Important

People with psychic powers generally believe that dreams can carry messages that can serve as a warning. To analyze your dreams start documenting them. The best way to do this is to maintain a dream diary kept next to your pillow. After you have documented a few dreams, try to find connections between them and check whether any part of your dreams has come true.

Try Following Your Gut Instincts

Have you ever felt peculiar about a place, event or person that you really can't put into words? Have you strongly felt that a certain situation might occur without having any evidence to back your feeling? These kinds of feelings are called gut instincts, and all of us have it in different degrees. Most people overlook their gut instincts and try to live their lives on the basis of rational thinking. Next time you have such a feeling, make a note of it and check if it actually comes true. Also try to determine if these feelings connect to your life in any way.

Always keep in mind that just because you have a gut feeling about something it doesn't really mean that it would come through. While it may come true, it could take months or even years for it to take place, which is why it will always help to make a note of these feelings so that when it happens you know for sure that you already knew about it.

Chapter 6: Experiences After The Opening Of The Third Eye

After your third eye opens you will go through some unusual experiences. While many of the experiences will be pleasant, there are some that might not be. If you feel some activity or pressure in the center of your forehead, it means that either your third eye has already opened or will open very soon.

Seeing Through The Third Eye

The Third Eye lets you to see past the visual images around you. With it, you can sense and visually interpret the energy around you. As you watch people walk in the park, you will grasp much more than just the abstract concept of random people walking in the park. You begin to see the interplay between the motion, energy, and intention in a vivid internal visual map. Life, therefore, becomes almost tangible to you.

While our physical eyes are blind to energy and can only see the results of energy, the Third Eye allows one to visualize where the energy is, to understand it and to actually see it. Our eyes are designed to see light while the third eye helps you process the energy you interact with in a precise manner.

Having an open Third Eye may seem like something mystical at first, but it merely is a new way that helps your mind communicate with the rest of your senses. This communication is direct and so uninhibited that you can accurately predict events and perceive potentials that are not physically present. This is a skill that is real that has been experienced by people from as early as the Paleolithic period.

What To Expect After The Third Eye Has Opened

After your third eye has opened, do not be surprised when you go through some unusual experiences. This will have a lot to do with what you see. For example when you are very tired after a long day's work and are about to sleep, you might see different kinds of images in the eye of your mind after you close your physical eyes.

Many of these images won't make a lot of sense and will be blurred or vivid. There are a number of dimensions you can reach with an opened third eye and you will experience them gradually. It all depends on your thought's vibration levels. The higher your vibration levels the more dimensions you will be able to explore. If you're seeing blurred visions, you will need to further strengthen your spiritual powers. Reaching a higher state of meditation will help you see more clearly with your third eye.

Higher And Lower Dimensions

If the vibrations of your thoughts are low then you will most likely see visions from a lower dimension. The lower dimension is the area where you will see restless souls. These are souls of the people who either killed themselves or could not forgive themselves for having done something in their lives. Since they are afraid of being judged they do not move into the higher dimension.

People who see visions from the lower dimension generally get scared of what they are seeing and regret opening their third eye. However, you don't have to remain in the lower dimension. Most people who remain at the lower dimension do so because the vibration created by their thoughts attracts this dimension. All you need to do is increase your vibration and step into a higher dimension.

If you would like to close your third eye, you can do so by avoiding spiritual practices, indulging in conversations that have nothing to do with the spiritual world and getting rid of every object in your surrounding that reminds you of it. While your third eye may not close immediately, slowly and gradually it will. However, it is important to note that once your third eye closes, it will take a lot of effort to open it back again.

With higher thought vibrations that include feelings of happiness, gratitude, love or peace you will be able to see more peaceful visions that would bring in a sense of fulfillment and relief to your soul. In this dimension, you will have visions of the hurt people go through and ideas that will help you make situations better along with feelings of compassion and forgiveness.

Sensitivity To Good And Bad Energies

Once your third eye has been awakened you'll become more sensitive to the energies of people around you. You will be able to detect between good and bad energies. It's always good to pick up good energies, because it will affect you positively. However, it is impossible not to pick up bad energies, which is why it's always good to avoid places where you know you will most likely to be hit by bad energies. This is one of the main reasons why people with stronger spiritual powers feel drained after spending time in a crowd, since they get hit by loads of bad energies.

When you're in the middle of bad energies try imagining being surrounded by positive energies in order to protect yourself. Think of something that makes you happy and continue to do so till you can get out of that atmosphere. It will stop your mind from being dragged into negative thoughts.

Once you're out of that situation and come back home, get under a shower with the water set to a slightly lower temperature than what you're used to. Imagine the water cleaning away all the bad energies that has affected you. As the water flows down from your body feel the bad energies flowing down with it. This is an excellent exercise to eliminate the effects of bad energy on your mind. As you do it for a couple of days, you will experience the cleansing effect more strongly. It will also help you become more focused and energetic throughout the day, and the ability of negative energies to disrupt your regular thought process will become weaker. It will also improve the quality of your life, your health, sleep, relationships and the general state of your mind.

Third Eye Opening Experiences

After your third eye has opened, during the initial period you might experience high-level vibrations that might scare you. The trick to get over this period is to stay calm and allow the vibrations to take control of your mind. As you stay calm, your mind will synchronize to the vibrations and will become accustomed to it.

You may see visions of beautiful places, which may include visions of a beautiful day or a beautiful house or anything that you feel is very peaceful and an enlightening place to be.

Even though you will not be at such a place physically, your mind will reap all the benefits of being in such a place. The vastness of the images that you see in your vision will vary on the level of focus and meditation that you have achieved. While for some the visions might be in a frame wherein the mind will be aware of the darkness that's around the frame, for some the vision would be frameless and the clarity will be so great that the mind will no longer see any darkness or troubled images.

Closing the Third eye

Many people may choose to shut their third eye. The experiences post awakening and activation of the third eye can be quite overwhelming for them. In such cases, the easiest way to keep it shut is to not use it at all. Opening the eye requires effort and changes in your normal life. If you do mundane and meaningless things that don't require the use of the third eye, it remains closed by itself. Just keep yourself focused on the regular stream of things.

For those who have opened their third eye, just push yourself back and become more grounded in the present. Keep bringing yourself to where you are and what is around you. Although you might start seeing and hearing more, you can control it. Just stop yourself from seeing or hearing the things you don't want to. It is as simple as closing your eyes when you don't want to watch something or skipping a channel on the television. Pay more attention to your physical presence and way of life. This will keep you grounded and prevent consciousness on higher levels. Don't drift your mind towards thoughts which are too deep and do not concern your daily life. All this helps to tone down the awareness of the third eye.

Chapter 7: FAQ's About The Third Eye

Who Has A Third Eye?

The Third Eye is natural to everybody. It is like a Meta-organ consisting of the mind and all other sense linked together and working cohesively and optimally. Everyone has access to this mystical eye. Even without training or refinement, the Third Eye gives us premonitions, or simply a hunch of what might happen. Therefore, everyone, whether he or she knows it or not, has at one or more times used the Third Eye.

Once opened and developed, the Third Eye gives you more insight than a mere hunch. It helps you clearly visualize the patterns of life that were previously hidden. This allows you to utilize all other organs maximally. In fact, those who have unlocked the mystical powers of the Third Eye use it in more ways than we can list here. Seers, for instance, will use it to see intricate connections and find answers to complex problems. Energy workers use it to consciously manipulate the energy around them for various purposes. You also unconsciously use your Third Eye when reaching out and touching other people's hearts through love or empathy.

Who Uses the Third Eye?

Essentially we all do. Each one of us has a Third Eye - the difference varies in the scope of what extent we choose to use it, whether we're aware or not that we are using it, and what frequency we exercise it to work for us to the nth degree.

Like any skill, there are a number of people who have a natural ability of tapping into the Third Eye's potential. Some of these people are called clairvoyants, seers, or gurus that are able to bring light to a confusing situation or block of some sort. Because their own minds are free of thought or clutter, they "see" clearly into a situation for a viable answer to emerge.

Any one of us can learn to do this too. It's a matter of practice, like training the body and mind for a particular vocation. Artists of all forms of media, who produce original works, whether it is music, video, literature or other, are actively using their Third Eye. The same goes for entrepreneurs and innovators in every field imaginable.

All of us have an imagination. It helps us solve problems more easily and create many of the things we see in our world today. The degree to which we use it aids to determine our way of living. How far we take it individually is a personal choice.

Is It The Same For Everyone?

Everyone has a Third Eye. Everyone can awaken and develop it. There's, however, a significant variance in the interpretation of the results of an open Third Eye. What you experience or see is highly subjective and varies from one person to another. In fact, experts agree that there is a lot of room for misinterpretation of the facts relayed to a person by the Third Eye.

Different people will see things differently. Likewise, what the Third Eye perceives will be different from one individual to another. What you visualize as a cup may mean something else to another person. This is why at times it gets very complicated to share with other people what you see with your Third Eye.

Since we are all human, nature has nonetheless made it possible for us all to push towards a common baseline. It is, therefore, right to say that commonalities do exist for people whose Third Eye is open. For example seeing auras is a mental capacity that the Third Eye confers to many folks. There are even experts who train people to view auras in a standard way.

There are numerous mystical practices that help people explore the different perceptions of life through the Third Eye. This, together with the unique nature of every person, means that what one sees through his or her Third Eye may be different from what is seen by someone else.

What Does The Third Eye Do?

The Third Eye is simply a sense. Like all your other senses, it, therefore, does nothing but relay information to you. Your eyes do not do anything active rather than transmitting visual information. Your ears are quite passive too; they merely convey auditory sensations to the brain. The same goes for all other sense organs. They all amass information and pass it on to the brain.

The Third Eye collects or perceives information about potential and the energy state around you. The information about potentials is all about what might be while the energy states are all about how things are being held around you. This information helps you to visualize people's emotions, how they are doing, their stories and even what lies ahead for them. You are additionally able to get an inkling of things that may be hidden from sight and even those that are yet to happen.

What You Need To Know?

Opening of the Third Eye has been described as a journey to enlightenment. Nevertheless, like all things, it has another side to it. With an open Third Eye, life is laid bare which means that you may see things that you did not wish to see. Before you embark on this mystic quest that allows you awaken your Third Eye, you must be ready to face whatever lies beyond ordinary sight.

The Third Eye is a natural skill and like all our skills, we can choose to use them for good or use them to commit evil. It is wonderful to experience a new dimension of life unknown to many. You must, however, be careful on how you use your power. Some people may be tempted to use it as a weapon to oppress, manipulate or even exploit. This is evil and far from the beauty that comes with developing the Third Eye.

One of the greatest risks of the Third Eye is that you can easily fall into delusion. If you get into it without proper guidance you may tip the balance between what is and what is not. The power of the Third Eye may, in the worst-case scenario, drive you insane. With proper training, however, you will be taught how control your power and how to maintain sane awareness of reality from the unreal.

What To Expect?

You must understand that many folks do not see the world through the Third Eye. When you experience your first vision, it may be all so new to you that you feel like a crazy drug trip. Telling it to other people just then may make things even worse. You may be persecuted and branded insane by people who do not quite understand what you are experiencing.

Your natural response may be to suppress this ability in order to prevent being made fun of or being labeled crazy. With enough suppression, the ability will eventually go away. Nevertheless, the Third Eye is an incredible mystical ability. You only need to take your time to learn and understand the process in a way that you do not think you are crazy. Once you understand the process, you will also be able to describe it to other people without sounding stupid.

Before you embark on a quest to unlock the mystical Third Eye, understand that you won't be getting concrete physical artifacts. The efficacy of Third Eye opening and development is entirely up to you. It is contingent on:

> The willingness to accept and pay attention to what your Third Eye connects you to
> Learning how to understand and accurately interpret what the Third Eye sees
> Being able to wisely act upon what you see

How Does An Awakened Third Eye Affect You?

Once you get better at meditating on your third eye, you will start noticing subtle changes. The more your third eye opens, the more vivid these experiences will be. You become more sensitive to all the energies around you. People always emit a sort of energy depending on their state of mind and being. As you become more perceptive of such things, you will be able to differentiate between the good and bad energies.

People with negative emotions like anger and hate will give off strong vibrations of bad energy. Those with a better state of mind will be the positive energies. As you are more receptive, the outside energies can also affect you. Good energy will leave you feeling rejuvenated while bad energy can make you feel completely drained. This is why you also need to learn to protect yourself and create a barrier between others and yourself.

Even when you are about to sleep, your mind is more receptive. You might suddenly see images without even thinking about it. These images might mean something to you while at times they might make no sense at all.

Blurred or hazy images appear more when you have just started honing the powers of your third eye. They become clearer as you get better at opening the third eye over time.

You will be able to see souls that are stuck between this word and the next. These are usually people who had unnatural deaths or felt they had some unfinished business. As a restless soul, they don't pass through to the next dimension after death. Such sights are visible when you open your third eye and your vibrations are at a level, which attracts them. Most people would choose not to be receptive to such images and thus work to reach a higher level.

At a higher level of awakening, you will be able to see beyond this world and can witness other dimensions. These often appear in bright light and vivid colors. It can often be too much for you to handle as well. The images of different dimensions might just overburden you. This is why you also need to learn to close the third eye in a subtle and slow manner. Allow yourself to shut these energies out and ground yourself to the present.

On a physical level, you will feel certain changes as you awaken your third eye. Headaches are common and can vary in intensity. While for some it is just a slight pressure on the forehead, others might experience a more intense sensation. However this passes after a while of practicing and is only an initial symptom of the opening. A more general feeling is a tingling sensation around your head, which stays for a while. All these symptoms are quite common when you begin meditation for the first time.

How Much Time Does It Take To Open The Third Eye

The time required for opening the third eye will vary for everyone. If you have some kind of spiritual experience in your childhood or have parents who are spiritually advanced, it will not take a lot of time to open your third eye. People who believe in past life feel that people who were spiritual in their past life will find it easier to open their third eye.

Opening your third eye might not immediately bring in pleasant visions and experiences. But as you practice meditation and continue to visualize through your third eye, you will be able to control it better and will reap the benefits of it. Many who attempt to open their third eye give up due to lack of patience not even realizing how close they were. If you begin working on opening your third eye, don't think of it as something you would like to do, but as something you must have, then you will surely achieve it.

Chapter 8 – Things You Should Know

In this chapter, I will discuss a few fun facts about your third eye that you probably didn't know but should.

The pineal gland, as I have told you before is located in nearly the direct center of your forehead. This gland habitually secretes the wonderful neurohormone melatonin while your body is in a state of rest at night. Scientists believe that this gland is one of the leftovers present in our body from the last vestiges of very early evolution.

Indeed, not getting enough rest and hence not letting the third eye work when it is time for it to work is causing a lot of people to develop chronic illnesses like Cancer. If you're unsure as to what I mean when I say that you are not letting your third eye get the proper rest, here is a list of the things you do that can potentially hamper your third eye from working properly:

Working in Artificial Light:

No matter how much your mobile phone manufacturer or computer manufacturer emphasizes that their technology makes the artificial light emanating from their devices makes it safe and viewable, truth is that working in artificial light is actively stopping your third eye from working properly and is giving you all sorts of ailments to boot!

Working Night Shifts:

Believe it or not, nights really are meant for sleeping and not for working. When you work all night, your eyes don't get rest. Yes, all three of them but even if you make up for your exhaustion by sleeping in the day, your pineal gland will not secrete the necessary melatonin and hence your third eye will not work in your favor or at all, for that matter.

Staying Up Too Late:

When you stay up too late, your eyes don't get rest. You disrupt your sleeping pattern and stop your pineal gland from functioning properly. Even if you stay up doing nothing, you are stopping your body from getting the rest it needs and hence stopping your third eye from working. This is the major reason why people suffering from insomnia will have more trouble opening their third eye as compared to people who have normal sleeping patterns.

Why Does This Happen?

Your pineal gland is directly related to the earths' rotatory patterns. By disrupting the pineal gland by indulging in the aforementioned points and by interrupting the melatonin's chronobiological connection to the earths' rotatory pattern, also known as its circadian rhythm, you are opening many doors. Yes, indeed. However, the doors you are opening are not those of perception but the terrible doors of diseases and ailments.

Recent studies have found there to be a connection between

disrupted circadian rhythms and heart disease, obesity as well as diabetes.

Studies conducted by the University of Michigan have revealed that the pineal gland is one of the most unexplored parts of the human body despite having been the subject of so much talk for so many decades. The reason behind this is the fact that the gland functions in ways that can only be described as mysterious. No one knows why a number of unique molecules are found in the pineal gland only at night and not in the day. Similarly, no one has been able to determine the exact pattern of the melatonin synthesis that occurs at night that is controlled by the superchiasmatic nucleus and is modulated by light.

Suffice it to say, the pineal gland works differently for every person and most of the guarantees you see in mainstream media are simply a result of pop culture or largely speculative at best.

However, the above being stated, here is a bit of a shortlist of the newer and more confirmed research relating to the pineal gland or the third eye.

The Third Eye Probably Started Off As A Real Eye:

Yes, indeed. Theories suggest that as the pineal gland acts as a sort of antenna or receptor for light and our retinas which might mean that the third eye started off as a real eye which either got absorbed into the brain with the passage of time after the other two eyes, I.e. the eyes we currently have evolved into our faces or whether it was simply an additional eye in the early stages of evolution with a spiritual and physical connection to the previous spiritual and physical evolutionary stages is still something both science and spirituality cannot quite seem to agree on.

The Earths' initial ancient cultural histories are somewhat filled with both one-eyed beings as well as three-eyed beings such as Shiva the Hindu god and Cyclops, the character appearing in numerous tales of folklore and even multiple religions throughout the world.

Not just in folklore and theory however, even though Homo sapiens' third eyes evolved into pineal glands, we still find many animals with photoreceptive third eyes that are more commonly referred to nowadays as parietal eyes. Furthermore, skulls and fossils found from other ancient creatures feature similar sockets in their skulls that can more or less prove the existence of a third eye.

Melatonin Regulates Your Life:

There is no doubt that the circadian patterns rule our lives but there is still no sure way to determine if our circadian pattern is on the right track. However, by observing melatonin secretion patterns, we can definitely see if a person' circadian patterns are on track or not.

Melatonin secretions help to heal our brain and align our bodies to the earths' rotations and research is being conducted on how to boost these secretions in order to help people combat various ailments.

Artificial Light Will Darken Your Future:

If you are someone worried about or combatting breast and prostate cancer, you might want to pay extra special attention to this. A recent study conducted by researchers at Harvard University concluded how our recent sleeping habitats have potentially increased our risks of getting cancer by 200%.

Studies have gone so far as to say that humanity has almost

completely blotted out the night sky. The research also noted that half the artificial light produced is wasted anyway.

Light at night has been proven to become a very high risk factor for a lot of diseases proven by a lot of researches conducted throughout the world. These researches were based on different people all around the globe proving the same point time and time again that artificial light at night contributes greatly to the risk factor of contracting hormonal cancer.

Studies have proven that the more women are exposed to artificial light at night, the higher their risk of breast cancer. A study found that going into average light from minimal light increased rate of breast cancer by 36% and going into more intense light brought the percentage up by a further 26%.

Up until a hundred years or so ago, the average American saw twelve hours each of daylight and night but now with the help of artificial lights, we've not only stretched the day but we've actively inserted light into our routine 24/7 in the shape of nightlights. Getting rid of these is easy enough and it can greatly improve your third eye chakras and stimulate melatonin production.

The Telly:

While I am not saying that the TV is your enemy, I'm not going to tell you that it is your friend either. Your TV doesn't just emit regular artificial light. It flickers, fluctuates and everything in between. Especially at night when your eyes are desperate for some rest, it pressurizes all three of your eyes and keeps melatonin production from going off-track.

Chapter 9 - Healing Your Third Eye

Take a moment to reflect back on the past few days. Are you constantly misplacing your belongings? Are you having trouble trying to visualize your last steps in order to find these belongings? If so is the case, your third eye chakra might be blocked.

If at any time you feel that your memory or imaginative skills are suffering, you might want to consider that your third eye or your third eye chakra is blocked. Memory and imagination are only two of the numerous cognitive functions that are handled by your third eye. A blocked third eye can prove bad for you in various ways. You can be anxious; you can suffer from headaches and will generally feel like you aren't in control of your surroundings. This is enough to make anyone's life miserable. However, there is no need to fret because here are a few things you can do in order to heal your third eye through various different ways:

How Do I Heal?

Just like healing any other aspect of your life, in order to heal your third eye chakra, you will need to first determine the cause or nature of the issue. There are usually two different types of third eye blockages. The first that is placed by you and the second that will be placed by people surrounding you.

Third Eye Blockages Placed By You:

Fear:

Fear is the most common type of blockages your chakra will face. If fear is the cause of your chakra's blockage, it is most likely because you are afraid of something you will see once your chakra has opened.

There is a lot of speculation about what happens when your third eye chakra opens.

'Will I see mutilated, dead bodies?' 'Will I see dead people walking around in various stages of decay?' 'Will I be able to turn the third eye off if I don't like what I see?' 'Once you open that floodgate, is there any way you can possibly go back to life as it was before?' 'Will I see tragedies and national disasters before they're about to take place?' 'Will I lose control of my mind and go completely crazy?'

What will happen if I see something bad? What will happen if I see something good?

If these are the questions that are plaguing you at night, stop right there. The best part about nature's gifts such as these is the fact that they can be stopped at will and that they are entirely within your control.

You will not have to see any of these things. Should you choose to accept this wonderful gift, it will be completely under your own control. You will be the master of what you see, when you see it and how you see it. You can do this by setting boundaries as in any other aspect of your life. You have boundaries as to who can approach you or call and text you in the middle of the night and the same applies for the gift.

If you feel like you don't want to be made aware of any sort of events before they occur, tell that to the gift. Say it loud and clear so that you and your chakra both are on the same page as to what you need.

You hold all the power when it comes to your third eye and hence all you need to do is decide how to use it.

All this being said, some people still manage to see bodies with various injuries, etc. walking around. The main thing to remember here is that these people were people like you not too long ago and hence there is no reason to be afraid of them. You must remember that most of the times, these people don't even realize that they are scaring someone walking around with their various injuries. They are usually, lost, confused and scared. The only difference between you and them is that they do not have a physical body any more.

In any case, if seeing these people is scaring you, you have the full authority to control them however you may wish to.

Lack of Self Belief:

After fear, the second largest cause for being unable to open your third eye is a lack of self-belief, i.e. lack in the faith that you can even do so.

Sometimes people believe that they have repaired their third eye beyond repair or that they don't simply have one. Keep in mind that this is the wrong approach and rather absurd as everyone has a pineal gland that is the third eye. Hence, you do, no matter what you have been led to believe for whatever reason, possess the third eye.

The only way to overcome this barrier is to unlearn everything you have ever learnt. Let go of every reservation and every previous concept you have about meditation and start to relax your mind. Let go of all reservations and start focusing on your pineal gland. Close your eyes if this helps. Don't be alarmed if you feel a pressure or warmth spreading from the center of your forehead and concentrate hard for an hour or so every day until you start to see some improvement and remember to believe in yourself.

Third Eye Blockages Placed By Others:

Control:

If someone has control over your life, it might prove to be difficult for you to practice your third eye experiments fully. You might even be aware of your psychic abilities but might still be unable to do something about it.

It might be someone apparent or it might be something you haven't even considered before. Maybe it's your brother? Maybe it's your father who has always been rather vocal about this sort of stuff and has blatantly refused to believe in it and has told you to stay away from it as well?

Or maybe it is the society you were raised in? A lot of religious folk deem the chakras and especially the third eye to be directly connected to satanic acts. However, the question arises, what power exists that can NOT be used for evil? The power is only as good or bad as the person using it. Remember that you know best of your intentions and if they are simply to explore your own power and your own minds realm then you have nothing to be afraid of.

However, all that being said and done, how do you release

these peoples' power from over you?

It's very simple. You tell them to stop. Yes, indeed. Remember that you are a free and liberated person and that using and exploring your third eye is in no way harmful to anyone. Make others understand this and if they don't, don't be afraid of any demonization they might channel unto you.

How Do I Tell if A Blockage Has Been Removed?

If you had been getting headaches that have suddenly stopped, rejoice because your blockage has been very likely removed.

If your imagination and dream activity is back to normal or has improved, your blockage has been removed.

You can ask your 'guides' to check for any chains and blockages during meditation and confirm that the blockage has been removed.

You can go to an energy healer or a shaman and ask them to check if your blockage has been removed. This is a very quick process.

Teas That Help Heal the Third Eye

If you are still unsure as to how you can heal your third eye, there are various numerous herbs and teas available that can help you boost your mental abilities and thus clear your third eye.

Here is a list of the ingredients you will need for the Third Eye Chakra Healing Tea:

Gotu Kola:

The scientific name for this herb is Centella Asiatica. This herb is to be used alongside Ginger. Gotu Kola has the unique ability that it can prepare your mind to be able to decipher the messages you are receiving. Gotu Kola strengthens your brain so that it can easily accept the load of the messages it is receiving and can process them and make rational thought out of them so your third eye doesn't get pressurized.

Even if you are just looking to optimize the mental functions, gotu kola is remarkably helpful in helping you increase brain activity. Additionally, it is beneficial for people suffering from Alzheimer's or those who have a family history of the same disease. It can also help prevent diseases of ageing such as Parkinson's, Dementia and various others. This herb also improves blood circulation all along the body so that your overall health will also improve when you take it simply in order to cleanse the mind and rid your third eye of any sort of pressure whatsoever.

Skullcap:

If you feel that you are receiving a jumble of many different and somewhat contradictory messages, you might want to consider using skullcap. Sometimes, our minds are not good at being able to decipher between the messages we are truly getting and the messages our ego is sending to us. This is when skullcap gets into the mix. Scutellaria Lateriflora is a wonderful herb that puts your mind at ease. It lets information flow freely and organically and also allows the messages to be understood in the context in which they are meant to be understood. If you have ADD or ADHD, you will most likely want to use this herb since it helps you to maintain a line of communication instead of going back and forth constantly.

Additionally, Skullcap can help you reduce all sorts of headaches and body pains as well. If anything, this herb will help you to let go of your body and reservations long enough that you can start to meditate without a care in the world so your third eye can open uninhibited until it become a norm and you can do so without the help of such herbs.

Nettle:

Nettle is an herb that should be used in conjunction with Skullcap. Urtica Dioica is one of the best herbs you can find on the market since it is one that has the most beneficial properties. It is also used as a tastemaker for various teas since it is so tasty.

Nettle is an extremely nourishing herb. Its uses are so versatile that you can use it in both teas as well as soup stocks. This is an herb that will nourish your mind to give it confidence without making you overconfident in the least. The plant of nettle stands tall and proud with tiny needles that make sure it is protected from predators and those who wish to harm it. Consuming tea made of the substance will pass on the same confident spirit unto your own body.

Ginger:

Zingiber Officinale turns your body into a receptor. Sometimes, your body can repel the third eye's energy. This is an unnatural function that must be gotten rid of in case you are to learn of the mystics and the mysterious ways of the third eye and practice intuition in your daily life. It is a preparatory herb that rids your body of the blockages and starts the current flowing through your veins. However, being a current simply is not enough and that is why you will need the Gotu Kola to help enhance your intuitive experience.

Other Herbs Worth Mentioning

Above we mentioned the teas you could use to aid you in your process of healing. Now, here are other herbs that can help you enhance as well as heal various aspects of your third eye so you can explore its potential to the fullest.

Passionflower:

You might feel it strange to see passionflower in this list but it can prove to be a great companion to healing and working with your third eye. Passionflower allows a restless mind to go into a deep sleep. This is why it is more commonly classified as a hypnotic. Here, I will debunk the myth that hypnotic herbs have anything to do with hypnotism. Hypnotic herbs, in fact, only get you more in touch with the spiritual realm and help your soul to transcend, momentarily, from the binds of the body.

Passionflower is a highly enabling herb that allows you to see and remember your dreams rather vividly. You will notice that as you grow old, your ability to remember dreams for long will lessen. In fact, it might start to fade the moment you wake up. Passionflower helps you to grasp on to your dreams and then hold on to them and analyze them.

However, sometimes the body starts to react negatively to these dreams due to fear or any other reason. Passionflower, being a sedative, helps the body remain relax so no harm comes to either the soul or the vessel as the flower works its magic and helps bring you safely back into the realm of the living. The herb is remarkable to help a person during an anxiety or panic attack during their spiritual journey.

Lemon Balm:

Though the purpose of the third eye is not to contact ghosts or loved ones who have since moved on, it can help do so by the use of lemon balm. If you are feeling nervous or anxious due to pressure on your third eye, lemon balm will help you relieve that stress and will also help the spirit you are reaching out to calm down.

When you have been connected with your loved one, Lemon balm will help forget old grievances and will help you mend rifts. It will help bring positive memories to the forefront of the mind so that you may be happy and make a pleasant experience out of the meeting.

This herb also has the remarkable properties of healing major skin and respiratory problems many of which are related to the blockage of the third eye chakra.

Sage:

You have probably heard of sage along with Witches' hazel in folklore and mythology but the fact is that this herb is one of the most powerful grounding herbs you can find. Sage is very good for clearing off any negative energy that might be affecting your system. It is also extremely helpful in clearing your chakras of negative vibes and to help you connect to your loved ones without any fault in the connection whatsoever.

It makes the first contact easier for both parties involved and it also keeps you from having a nervous breakdown due to so much energy passing through your system. It is also good for meditating.

Gingko:

Gingko Biloba is a nervine that is used in medicines all around the world. It has some of the same characteristics as Gotu Kola that is why they both complement each other so wonderfully. When united, these herbs can prove to make quite a powerful concoction that can give your brain a jolt and help it to work clearly.

Nervines help make the nervous system strong so it can handle added amounts of stress. These herbs are used to alleviate stress and can help you to improve your memory and help you perform better under various degrees of stress. Nervines can also help you get rid of headaches that become a very common problem if you have a blocked third eye chakra.

Chapter 10 - Feeding your Chakra for Increased Intuition

The Third eye chakra can help us to move from the micro-observation to the macro-observation of all that is. This means the present, definitely but also the past stages of evolution as well as the future in the form of intuition.

If nothing else, you should be interested in freeing this chakra because it helps you to live a better and peaceful life on the basis of the best sort of intuition. Sometimes this intuition speaks to us as clearly as if someone were standing beside us whispering into our ears at the very same time. Others, it helps steer us gently through whispers and signs we have to actually look for. Whatever the case may be, the third eye chakra is a valuable asset and even if we don't plan on using the chakra's powers, it is a good idea to rid our penial glands of any sort of pressure that come to it during our daily lives so as to live a stress free life.

When it comes to food, unfortunately we have long since forgotten how to eat, what to eat and how much to eat in order to make our bodies and our souls healthy. We know only to consume to fill and in today's time and age, it is not exactly surprising that we are finding an easy way out in our foods as well.

How To Eat Healthy To Help Our Chakra:

Eat Intuitively:

If your body wants something, chances are, it needs it to remain healthy, given that it is not a substance you are abusing. Human beings are intuitive but sometimes we let our intellect take the wheel and we force ourselves to eat stuff that our body doesn't want or need simply because we think we know better. By tuning into the radio that is our souls and by listening to our soul and its needs, we can make sure that everything we consume is actually healthy for us. Pay attention to your soul and what it says when you're hungry. If you feel that you need more protein and thus would like to have some eggs, do that. Additionally, if you feel that your body needs to build up on calcium, don't wait until your teeth and bones start to hurt. Start making up on milk intake and even some daily use calcium tablets.

Remember the more you listen to your body, the more it will be willing to talk to you!

Nourish the Brain:

The brain is one of the most essential organs of the body and needs nourishment like any other organ. About 60% of the brain is fat. How can we turn this fat healthy? By feeding it healthier fats or foods that promote healthy fat building. You can get these fats from natural and unsaturated sources such as fish, nuts, seeds, some grains and omega-3 fats. Consuming these fats will ensure that your body is functioning properly without you getting obese and that your brain is working to optimum efficiency as well. These fats will also help you get into and maintain a positive mood throughout the day until it becomes more or less a norm. Studies have shown that people who have depression have lesser amounts of Omega-3 fatty acids in their blood that keeps them from absorbing the endorphins their body produces to the fullest amount which results in lethargy as well as depression. Eat better fats in order to assure that your body has all the

Eat Well To Sleep:

Admit it, you've been there. Call it a new phenomenon or call it a new disease but the easy living lifestyle has given us all the nighttime eating syndrome disorder. This is where a person spends night at home instead of out participating in other activities and consequently fills their bodies with various snacks and other meaningless carbs that keep the body from getting hungry but also keep it from getting the nutrition it truly needs. Even if you do have a proper meal, chances are that you will be indulging in post-dinner snacks and if you have these too close to bedtime, you will more than likely disrupt your sleeping pattern. If we have a snack right before bed, we will send our third eye into an overactive mode where it will keep us up and from our precious melatonin cycle and will also keep us from getting a good night's sleep.

If you want a good night's rest that actually helps you to relax and wake up rejuvenated, curtail nighttime eating.

What Foods Help Improve Your Third Eye

Chocolate:

Rejoice! Chocolate is one of the most powerful foods for the third eye chakra – its vibration replenishes and stimulates this center, and it does so in a number of ways. Dark chocolate contains caffeine that stimulates the brain and thinking, enabling us to focus on a task at hand better. This means that not only will your chakra open up, you will also be able to focus better on multiple tasks at hand. It also contains antioxidants known as flavonoids that help to open us the blood vessels. Antioxidants can help release harmful toxins from our bodies and help us to live healthier lives. They also prevent breakouts of the skin and overall make our skin look better in many different ways and also give the skin a better glow. You may even become more relaxed and lower your blood pressure as a result of this effect. Aside from its physiological effects, it can certainly alter your psychology – our mood, as it contains several constituents that act as stimulants or that give us the comforting "I'm in love" feeling. These are the same endorphins that help you remain happy throughout the day. Hence pair chocolate with Omega-3 fatty acids in order to attain full affect. Try having a small square of dark chocolate in the late afternoon to help your brain to revive from thinking all day long and to help your mood sink into one of relaxation. Remember that the darker the chocolate, the healthier it is. Milky chocolate has added sugars that might give you a buzz but it will not help your third eye. Forego big brand names that try and sell you dark chocolate that is only made dark with the help of food coloring. Instead, opt for raw chocolate or cooking chocolate that is less processed and hence closer to the real deal, the thing you are looking for.

Spice of Life:

Spices help increase your metabolism meaning that your body will digest and utilize fats faster. Sometimes, it's as simple as increasing the spices in your foods before your body kicks itself and starts digesting the fats you had been trying to lose for such a long time.

However, when it comes to intuition, remember that it is intense which is also the deal with spices. If you've ever gotten an odd sort of piercing feeling whilst consuming spices, that is because due to their pungent nature, spices dissolve into your blood and directly affect your third eye. Talk about eye-openers! Spices are not only good for flavor but they also help to stop the brain from ageing. They keep intellect sharp and help improve memory.

Curry spice is especially one of the most beneficial spices because it helps improve cognitive movements which are directly associated with the third eye. It also contains antioxidants that help a person to reduce the toxins in their bloodstream and live healthily. What's more, they help reduce the bad fats and proteins in the blood that directly affect the brain and cause dementia in patients.

Purple Berries:

These are not to be mixed with blueberries. These berries can help your body get more antioxidants than chocolate and hence can boost the cleansing of your system. Studies have shown that while other foods might prevent ageing, these berries can actually help one to reverse ageing and show cognitive improvements! Apart from these, blueberries and strawberries help to improve brain function and boost both learning as well as memory. You can have these as a raw snack or in smoothies for full effect.

Chapter 11 - Some Facts About The Third Eye

Here are some facts that you may previously not have known about the third eye chakra and what it does for your body:

The Color:

The color associated with the third eye is that of the color indigo. If you sometimes feel concentration whilst meditation to be waning, simply light a candle of this color. Additionally, you can start wearing indigo clothing whilst you are concentrating on focusing on the third eye, as this will keep you focused and on track. Sometimes surrounding yourself with flowers of this color can also help a person to stay focused.

Crystal Therapy:

Some people find that crystal therapy is a good way to meditate in order to activate the third eye. While this is not absolutely necessary, here is a list of the crystals that are most commonly associated with the third eye and thus can help you meditate and open your pathway more easily:

Purple fluorite

Sugilite,

Lapis Luzuli
Amethyst

Aquamarine

Clear Quartz

Lolite, Azurite

Angelate

Sodalite

Aqua Aura Crystal

Blue Aventurine

Dumortierite

Axinite

Chiastolite

Blue Aragonite

Cacoxenite

Lazulite

Merlinite

Ulexite

Blue Tourmaline

Phenacite

Stilbite.

Aromatherapy for the third eye:

If you find that you wish to meditate and stimulate meditation further, you may do so by aromatherapy. This can be done by burning incense or via perfumes and even perfumed candles. However, be warned that if you do this immediately before sleeping, your brain cells will become active and will start to get stimulated thus sending your brain into overdrive. Hence, aromatherapy should always be done in the morning or early evening hours so as not to disrupt your sleeping pattern in any way.

Here are the smells that can help stimulate your third eye:

Angelic Root

Bay Laurel

Clary sage

Cypress

Elimi

Frankincense

Helichrysum

Juniper

Marjoram

Patchouli

Rosemary

Sandalwood

Vetiver

Sounds That Stimulate the Third Eye:

Every chakra has a specific sound that helps the meditator to concentrate on meditation by driving thoughts out verbally. The sound for the third eye chakra is 'Eem' and it resonates with the phonics of the alphabet: 'A'.

Healing Your Third Eye With Nature:

You came from nature and to it you will return. Don't confine yourself to the four walls of your home for long periods of time. If you feel that you cannot concentrate, go out to be one with nature.

Go out and pick a spot away from human signs. Sit on a mat and meditate. Turn your face towards the sun and close your eyes. Feel the sunlight enter you through your forehead and resonate in the form of energy throughout your body.

Chapter 12 – Common Problems Faced

If you are struggling with opening your third eye chakra, here are 4 of the most common traps you will need to avoid in order to open your chakra fully:

Giving Up Too Easily:

When it comes to your chakra, the sky is the limit. Don't let yourself give up because you might be mere inches from the finish line. Remember to keep on going. Sometimes, it will be scary until you realize that it is your power to do with it as you so wish. Don't let anything scare you from your goal of exploring your mind and keep working hard towards your goals.

Holding on To Old Habits:

Don't be stubborn. Unlearn everything you think you know. Chances are that if the eye isn't opening, it is because you are holding on to a habit that you think is harmless. Is it a piece of logic you think will help your spiritual journey? Is it insecurity or do you not believe that you will succeed in your endeavors? Whatever the case, don't hold on to old habits and start letting go. The sooner you do this, the sooner your third eye will open and work along to your wishes.

Being Too Energetic:

Don't open your chakra after you down three cans of energy drink. Don't jump up and down. Don't over stimulate yourself because that can cause your connection to become jerky at best and will cause you to get exhausted quickly. Similarly, don't push yourself to do something your body isn't ready for yet. If your body thinks it can't handle talking to your deceased loved ones tonight, listen to it. Don't force yourself to indulge in something you're not ready for because the only one suffering will be you.

Getting Lost In The Realms:

What you might read right now might seem a bit contradictory but it's true. There is a wrong way to meditate. Remember that you belong in this realm no matter how much tempting the other might seem. You are not supposed to use this as an escape from this reality and any problems you might be facing right here.

Don't be fooled, if you want to find a means of escape, you will likely find a nice nook or cranny where you can hide from your real life but remember that you are on this plane of existence for a reason and you belong here and not there. When you leave here, you leave your vessel in neglect and hence you might not be able to handle it when you come back so take this step very wisely.

Chapter 13 - 7 Steps To Increase Your Clairvoyant Power

What image comes to mind when you hear the words psychic? When most people think of a psychic, they probably imagine an exotic-looking woman gazing intently into a crystal ball. She is probably wearing giant hoop earrings and a long, flowing dress. She might speak in a rather hoarse tone and with a foreign accent relay your future as she tries to look through the mist that becomes clear as soon as you pay her.

However, if you have been following me on my journey throughout this book, I can assure you that you can be your own clairvoyant. Here is how:

These experiences of clairvoyance are quite normal and often very useful. I am now going to teach you how to practice and improve on these experiences until they become the norm and you become quite adept at controlling your clairvoyance yourself.

We enhance and improve clairvoyance, like any behavior,

with learning and practice. If you follow the seven steps listed below and practice them for seven days in a row, you'll experience more consistent and reliable clairvoyant images.

STEP 1: Release the Fears of Seeing the Future.
Remember when I said that you need to remove the fear blockage? Fear blockages usually occur during early childhood because children are so afraid of what they see. This is a great pity since children are innocent and hence souls and bodies are more comfortable revealing themselves to children.

However, children often "turn off" their clairvoyance because of fear. This fear could come from a thoughtless remark by adults who say the child's invisible friend is his imagination (when, in truth, the child is seeing angels and spirit guides). Sometimes, parents tell their children that psychic insights are evil. Or, the child may see a frightening image of her parent's impending divorce, or some other painful future event. She then shuts her clairvoyant vision, because she doesn't want to see her future.

Whatever the source of fear, we must release this emotion to regain our full clairvoyant power. One of the best ways to rid yourself of fear-blocks is through saying an affirmative phrase. Sit in a comfortable position and take two or three very deep and slow breaths. Tell yourself, aloud, that you are not afraid of anything and are willing to open your third eye to improve clairvoyance.

STEP 2: Know What You Want To Know:

Carefully word your questions so you'll receive an answer that truly meets your needs. The best way is to be honest with yourself about your "bottom line" true desires.

Don't be shy to ask for what you want. If you want to know whether you'll run into someone you like at the club, ask that. Remember that this is serious business and the third eye does not care for shyness and any sort of fooling around. You will get an honest answer only if you ask an honest question hence ask for what you want and clearly.

STEP 3: Breathe and Concentrate Upon Your "Third Eye".

After asking your question, take three deep and slow breaths. Put your focus on the area between your two eyes. This is an energy center, known as a your third eye. This is where your penial gland is located which activates clairvoyance. This is the gland that will help facilitate psychic pictures in answer to your questions.

At this stage, some people actually visualize a real eye resting between their eyebrows. This is the third eye choosing to reveal itself. Notice whether this "third eye" has its eyelid closed, open, or partially open. If the eyelid is closed or partially closed, ask it to open. Again ask the eye to open by clearing with yourself that you want this more than anything. When the eye opens, you will be rewarded with a great surge of power and warmness as well.

STEP 4: Notice any Pictures

Clairvoyant images generally come in one of four ways:

As a single picture inside your mind's eye

As a single picture that you see outside your mind's eye

As a movie image inside your head

or a movie image outside your head. The pictures can be black and white or full color. Sometimes, they may appear as a painting or a cartoon.

Remember that these are merely signs that you will have to interpret as meanings. Try and remember every detail you can at this point since you will be deciphering the meanings of these images after weeks to come since these prophecies can span over years of time.

STEP 5: Trust in What You See.

This last step is crucial, because if you discount your clairvoyant images or write them off as mere imagination, they are lost opportunities. You'll gain more confidence in your psychic abilities if you keep a record of your clairvoyant images. Try and increase your memory and remember these images so that you will be able to progress on to the next parts of the process that will make this whole ordeal easier for you gradually.

STEP 6: Control the Images:

This step will work for you like a computer where you will be able to control these images and make them bigger and enlarge them so you can see them in high resolution. You will also be able to save these images in your mind so that you may later pull these out and look at them when need be. This however is a stage that will only come to you through weeks of practice but if you keep true to it, it will come.

STEP 7: Command the Images:

This is the last stage and the one that every clairvoyant hopes to achieve. In this stage, you will be able to channel your images into a crystal ball. Hence, these images will not remain images but will become a sequence and even a moving picture in some cases. This is a process that can take months or even years depending on how much you have concentrated over the process and worked for it practically. However, don't imagine that this will happen the day you start meditating. This is a gradual process that takes time but is worth the fruit it reaps in the end.

How To Use The Melatonin Secreted By The Third Eye

The third-eye governs intuition, wisdom and clairvoyance. It sits in the middle of your brow just above your eyes and is associated with the color indigo

Amazing sex happens when we give ourselves permission to trust our intuition and connect on a deeper level beyond what is visible in the physical realm. When the third eye is clear, we can find ourselves flowing in harmony with our sexual partners, but when it's blocked, we may struggle to reach this degree of intimacy.

As I have previously discussed, the penial gland secretes melatonin that improves cognitive functions. Melatonin was previously known to cause the skins of amphibians to blanch, but its functions in mammals remained uncertain until research discoveries in the 1970s and '80s suggested that it regulates both sleeping cycles and the hormonal changes that usher in sexual maturity during adolescence.

The pineal gland's production of melatonin varies both with the time of day and with age; production of melatonin is dramatically increased during the nighttime hours and falls off during the day, and melatonin levels are much higher in children under age seven than in adolescents and are lower still in adults.

Melatonin apparently acts to keep a child's body from undergoing sexual maturation, since sex hormones such as luteotropin, which play a role in the development of sexual organs, emerge only after melatonin levels have declined.

This hypothesis is supported by the fact that children with tumors of the pineal gland often reach sexual maturity unusually early in life, presumably because the pineal's production of melatonin has been hampered.

Melatonin also seems to play an important role in regulating sleeping cycles; test subjects injected with the hormone become sleepy, suggesting that the increased production of melatonin coincident with nightfall acts as a fundamental mechanism for making people sleepy. With dawn the pineal gland stops producing melatonin, and wakefulness and alertness ensue.

The high level of melatonin production in young children may explain their tendency to sleep longer than adults.

However, it is interesting to note here that in mammals other than humans, melatonin possibly acts as a breeding and mating cue, since it is produced in greater amounts in response to the longer nights of winter and less so during summer.

Animals who time their mating or breeding to coincide with favorable seasons (such as spring) may depend on melatonin.

Here are five benefits of melatonin for human beings other than a good night's sleep:

More melatonin, less PMS

If you are a woman and suffer from PMS, you might often find yourself in a weird situation where you are pulling your hair out for no reason. If that is the case, take a look at your sleep habits. A study by different researchers has shown that low melatonin levels play a role in <u>premenstrual dysphoric disorder</u> (PMDD), or good old fashioned PMS. However, if you think you're in a bad mood for just ONE week of the month, think again. Chances are, your hormonal mood swings are making people run for cover even during the month no matter where the moon or your period is standing.

Stop The Clocks

Yes, indeed. Melatonin can effectively stop the ageing clock and even send it running backwards! Though the process does not slow down by a huge amount, it does slow down significantly enough to make you feel healthy and keep your skin glowing and fresh. That's good, right?

Stay Slim

Melatonin will help you keep slim. The process is rather simple and very uncomplicated. What happens is that you get enough sleep and hence do not crave the sugars you would otherwise in order to stay awake. Hence, this would keep you active and burn fat while stopping you from consuming more and thus increasing your belt size.

Get Rid of Migraines

If you stay up too late too often, you will be likely to have migraines. Melatonin can help reduce these migraines significantly. A research conducted found that "Three mg of melatonin was more effective than the placebo and had efficacy similar to that of 25 mg of amitriptyline, a common sleep aid and antidepressant. Furthermore, it was better tolerated than amitriptyline, with lower rates of daytime sleepiness and no weight gain." This means that even by just getting good sleep via meditation, you can avoid migraines completely. Focus on opening your third eye in order to improve melatonin secretions.

Get Rid of a Slow Thyroid

When you don't sleep enough, your body slows down a LOT. This means melatonin production as well. This can lead to serious thyroid disorders that can promote obesity and slow down metabolism in your body. Keep a check on this by getting melatonin supplements as well as getting enough sleep.

Research has proved that melatonin not only decreases depression and belly fat but it also helps to improve metabolism and overall productivity. Open your third eye to reap all these benefits for free and without the harmful side effects of the supplements.

Chapter 14 - Activating the Third Eye Through Body Purification

There is a common misconception about the third eye that frequently prevents a lot of people from activating it and accessing all of its hidden powers. This misconception is that the third eye can only be activated through yoga and meditation. Remember, the third eye is not based in mysticism; it is not an abstract concept. Your third is a metaphysical part of your body that has an actual impact on your physical health, particularly your pineal gland. It may not possess physical presence but it does have an effect on your physical wellbeing.

This means that your third eye does not necessarily have to be activated using spiritual triggers. It can be activated through alterations in your physical self as well, particularly activities that improve the functioning of the pineal gland. In fact, applying physical techniques that open your third eye might actually help you to implement spiritual techniques more effectively. You'd essentially be washing your own hands twice; doing so will only make them twice as clean, so why not go for it! In order to help you activate your chakra using natural and physical alterations to your lifestyle, what follows is a list of things you can do.

Avoid Fluoride

Fluoride is not at all good for you, this much is certain. Consuming it actually prevents calcium from strengthening your bones, so you should avoid this chemical from a purely medical perspective. Fluoride also damages your pineal gland, which means that consuming fluoride will make it exceedingly difficult for you to activate your third eye no matter how much you meditate. Hence, in order to prevent your hard fought meditation from going to waste, it is highly recommend that you avoid fluoride in all things from the food you consume to the water you bathe in!

This may seem difficult at first. After all, many cities have started to fluoridate their water in order to ensure that children get fluoride to strengthen their teeth. This misguided policy will force you to consume a lot of fluoride. The best thing you can do is to get a water filtration system installed. It will leach all of the fluoride out of your water, thereby removing a great deal of fluoride from your daily diet! Of course, the very first step you should take is to cut fluoride toothpaste out of your daily routine completely.

Quitting such things that have become an important part of your everyday will be difficult, and getting a water filtration system installed will be both costly and time consuming, but trust me when I say that it will greatly benefit you in the long run. You will begin to see results almost instantaneously, as your meditation will become increasingly effective as your body gets used to not being full of fluoride. When you start feeling the strength and wisdom of your third eye flowing through you, you will realize that all of the effort that you had to put into cutting fluoride out of your life was truly worth it!

Go For the Source

As has been mentioned already, the pineal gland has a lot to do with the third eye and vice versa. Hence, logic dictates that if you alter your routine to improve the functioning and health of your pineal gland you will be improving the effectiveness of your meditation and yoga as well. There are several techniques you can use to improve the functioning of your pineal gland, a lot of which do not require you to practice any form of yoga or meditation whatsoever!

One great way that you can improve the functioning of your pineal gland is to start consuming pineal gland stimulants and detoxifiers. These stimulants and detoxifiers are essentially chemicals and trace nutrients that are naturally present in several foods. Your body can uses these chemicals and nutrients to specifically boost the functioning of your pineal gland, thereby making it a lot easier for you to activate your third eye. There are a wide variety of nutrients and chemicals that can be considered pineal gland boosters and detoxifiers.

These include:

Chlorella

Blue-green Algae

Zeolite

Hydrilla Verticillata

Spirulina

Iodine

Zeolite

Ginseng

Blue Skate Liver Oil

Chlorophyll

Bentonite Clay

Vitamin D3

Borax

You can consume a lot of these stimulants on their own. Chlorophyll, for example, can be purchased separately and consumed just like any other supplement. The same goes for blue skate liver oil and many other stimulants in that list. Other stimulants can be found in several foods. Iodine, for example, can be consumed by using iodine salt instead of regular table salt. Vitamin D3 can be found in milk. Altering your diet to include these supplements can really improve your activation rate for your third eye.

Detoxify Your Body

The activation of your third eye is not based solely in trace nutrients and supplements either. There are foods you can eat that cover a wide range of nutrients that boost the functioning of your pineal gland and, as a result, help you to activate your third eye in a more efficient manner as well.

There are several special foods that you can incorporate into your diet which would help you to activate your third eye. The vast majority of these foods work by detoxifying your body, thereby making it easier for your prana to flow through you and reach your third eye. Remember, a toxic body is not a conducive environment for spiritual growth. Your prana needs a clean network of roads within you in order to travel to your chakras. Hence, one of the best ways in which you can activate your third eye is to detoxify your body using these foods.

One excellent food, or drink technically, that you can consume is apple cider vinegar. Raw apple cider vinegar works best because it would not possess any additives that would limit its effectiveness. Apple cider vinegar flushes your body of toxins in an extremely efficient manner, so consuming two tablespoons a day, one after waking up and one right before sleeping, can do a lot to detoxify your body.

There is another magic potion that you can drink in order to detoxify your body in a very efficient manner. This "magic potion" is the juice of the noni berry. This juice is delicious and extremely good for your health, but it is very strong so don't have more than a few tablespoons a day. Remember, too much of a good thing can be dangerous.

Incorporate Healthy Oils

Traditional yogic practice involves heavy use of oils. Oils possess detoxifying chemicals in extreme concentration as long as they have been manufactured in a pure and toxin free environment. Hence, incorporating these oils into your daily life can help you enter into a state of deep spiritual well being and thus activate your third eye. Using these oils greatly boosts the flow of prana in your body, and a speedy flow of prana reaching your third eye means that it will begin to activate, filling you with the knowledge of past lives and the universal wisdom that is inherent in all mankind.

Lavender, sandalwood, frankincense, parsley, oils derived from all of these materials can be greatly beneficial to anyone who is looking to activate their third eye. Try adding them to your bathwater, bathing and absorbing its heat and meditating straight after. You are going to feel all of the roadblocks that you would normally feel simply drift out of your way. This is because one of the most important things that these oils do is that they relax your muscles and sore any aches and pains you may have. Removing physical distractions from your own body will leave your mind free to wander the path of enlightenment.

These oils are so powerful that using them whilst meditating can allow you to accomplish feats such as astral projection. If you burn these oils in a nebulizer while meditating you may find yourself connected to a cosmic awareness. Many people who use these oils regularly report feeling a disconnection from self and reconnection with a greater power. This often involves a complete separation of body and consciousness, with some people even reporting seeing incredibly visuals of planetary systems and past lives.

Use the Sun

The energy that the earth receives from the sun is extremely powerful. Traditional Hindu belief states that the sun is the physical manifestation of God in this dimension, a kind of representation that is somehow conceivable by our fragile minds. The sun does give life to everything on our planet, including us, so there is much credibility to this belief.

Using the energy that the sun provides can be extremely beneficial to your efforts at activating your third eye. There are several ways in which you can use solar energy in order to activate your third eye and boost the flow of prana within your body. The first and most obvious way is, of course, to sunbathe. Your body can absorb solar energy through your skin without you having to put in any extra effort. The most effective use of solar energy in this manner is to do yoga in sunlight.

Yoga increases the flow of prana within your body, as does the absorption of solar energy through your skin. Hence, doing yoga while sunbathing is an extremely efficient way to direct the prana of your inner spiritual network towards your third eye. You can also meditate whilst sunbathing after you have completed your yoga routine. Yoga makes prana flow through your body, solar energy boosts the flow of prana and through meditation you can direct your prana to your third eye.

The energy of the sun is most powerful at sunrise and sunset, which works beautifully in your favor because these times are when the heat of the sun is the least oppressive. You can take this opportunity to gaze at the sun as well during the first fifteen minutes of sunrise and last fifteen minutes of sunset to direct solar energy through your ocular nerves into your third eye.

Incorporate Chants into your Meditation

There is a lot of skepticism even in the spiritual community regarding chanting. Many people simply don't understand the purpose of chanting, and believe that it is just a leftover practice from an ancient religion that is no longer relevant. What these skeptics fail to realize is that this ancient religion had discovered truths about ourselves that science has only just begun to realize.

Hence, it is only logical to assume that chanting does have a tangible affect on our bodies. Indeed, this assumption is actually correct. Chanting is essentially a drone originating from our vocal chords that is released from the body through our nose, as long as you are chanting right and keeping your mouth closed. Sound is created through vibrations, so when you chant you are causing vibrations through reverberate throughout your nasal cavity and the entire front of your face.

This causes your tetrahedron bone to vibrate. As it turns out, when your tetrahedron bone vibrates your pineal gland is stimulated, which of course helps to activate your third eye. In fact, the hormones that are released when you chant actually help you to stay young because of two reasons. Firstly, your third eye is activated and the flow of prana within your body is regulated. This naturally slows down the aging process because your body is able to withstand a lot more wear and tear.

The second reason is that the hormones released during chanting actually helps your body to regulate the various functions that it must perform in order to stay alive. When these functions become more efficient, your body is no longer put under as much stress as it was before and, as a result, the process of ageing slows down automatically. So do yourself a favor and incorporate those chants into your meditation!

Use Crystals

Crystals are an extremely important and useful way to align your chakras and activate your third eye. They adjust the frequencies of your prana by attuning your physical self to the vibrations of the universe, therefore allowing you to commune with the cosmic consciousness and see into the soul of the universe. It is a truly unique way to experience God, and is a highly recommended solution if you are feeling depressed or low in any way.

Amethyst, sodalite and rhodonite are great choices if you are going to start using crystals to activate your chakras. They work by providing energy to your third eye via your pineal gland. They act essentially like magnifying glasses, providing the energy you are directing towards your third eye with a catalyst of sorts that can purify the energy and make it more palatable for your body.

Remember, the energy you are absorbing can sometimes be impure or unclean, and as a result might make you ill. The best way to clean it is to channel it through crystals.

You can use crystals to aid you in your quest to activate your third eye by lying down on your back and placing the crystal between your two physical eyes, essentially where your third eye is supposed to be. Meditate for about fifteen minutes while the crystal is on your head, and try to do so under the light of the sun.

You already know how powerful solar energy is, imagine how effective it will be if it is magnified through healing crystals! If you mix chants into your meditation, you will have yourself an incredibly efficient way to activate your third eye and finally meet your spirit guide.

Use Magnets

Magnets are an often overlooked asset in the world of meditation. People are very fond of using crystals but for some reason magnets do not possess the same sort of appeal. However, it is highly recommended that you try using magnets simply because they are so incredibly effective!

Magnets work by decalcifying your third eye. You might not realize it, but having been inactive for so long has made your third eye very rusty. Imagine if you don't drive your car for decades, it would be a miracle if it worked without you having to make some serious repairs!

Magnets also work by leaching acidity from the area where they have been placed. Acidity is the bane of prana, so if you want to achieve a consistent flow you will need to cut all acidity from your body. Magnets allow you to do this in a very efficient way by making the area upon which they have been placed alkaline.

In order to use magnets, you must place the magnet upon your third eye similar to how you would place a crystal. Where a crystal would magnify the energy you are channeling to your third eye, magnets work by cleaning out your third eye to make it more receptive to energy. You do not need to meditate during this procedure, in fact it is recommended that you don't. Let the flow of energy be still as your third eye is purified.

Doing this therapy under the light of the sun will double its effectiveness. Solar power is a great catalyst, which means that if you lie under the sun with a magnet on your forehead you will actually be making it a lot easier for you to open your third eye!

Remove Acids from your Diet

As is mentioned in the previous section, acids are very bad for your prana. This is because they make your entire internal system sluggish, thereby disrupting the flow of energy. In a way, they make the roads, or channels rather, that your energy uses to travel a lot smaller. This means that less energy gets through and blockages emerge.

In order to prevent this from happening you obviously need to remove acid from your body. Magnets help you to do this, but it would also help if you do not consume acids in the first place. Cutting acids out of your diet, at least wherever it is possible without harming your health, will clear up the pathways for your prana to flow.

Remember, no matter how much you meditate if your pathways are not clear you will simply not be able to get the same results. In fact, if you meditate without clearing up the channels of prana first, you will probably end up causing a major blockage.

This is very dangerous, as it can cause some serious health

problems. Too much prana getting backed up in an area of your body can cause over stimulation of your endocrine glands, causing conditions such as hyperthyroidism.

Hence, if you are going to start meditating to activate your third eye, make sure you spend some time taking the acids out of your diet and your body. It will be healthier for you in the long run, and will help to make the process of activating your third eye a lot easier!

Be Diverse

These tips are pretty general, which means that they can be followed by pretty much anybody. However, it is not all that uncommon for people with certain specific spiritual requirements to get less than satisfactory results from a lot of these techniques.

This is because everybody has a different physical and spiritual make up. Some people just don't have the spiritual energy to be able to activate the third eye without using crystals. For other people, using crystals causes overstimulation and a great amount of discomfort as a result. Just remember that none of these techniques are set in stone. Some will work for you, some might not, and if you are experiencing difficult just remember that it is not your fault.

Try different things, be flexible about your meditative habits and before you know you will have made some great progress in your quest to activate your third eye.

Chapter 15 - Why Should You Activate Your Third Eye?

The most valid question you can ask during the entire process of activating your third eye and contacting the spirits that can provide you with guidance is why? Why should you put all of this effort in to activating an eye that has no physical presence on your body? What benefits can you derive from all of this meditating and yoga, what benefits will activate your third eye give you anyway?

If you are asking yourself these questions, know that you are going through a very important phase in your spiritual journey. If you coast through your spiritual awakening you might not have done things right, because in order to fully awaken yourself to the cosmic consciousness your third eye connects you to you must understand why you are activating your third eye in the first place.

Understanding the why helps you to understand the implications of the task that you are undertaking. This will allow you to put in the amount of effort necessary, and to grasp the consequences of what will happen if you are able to successfully activate your third eye. Here is a list of reasons that will help you understand why you are on this journey. Your third eye's connection to your spirit guide plays an important part in all of these reasons!

Discover Your Purpose

Nowadays, humanity is a species that is adrift. We have solved the problem of trying to survive in a hostile environment by becoming the masters of that environment. Once survival was no longer a problem, we set out to make the acquisition of luxury as easy as possible. We made our lives as easy as we possibly could. Now we are connected to each other through technology, but we have lost our sense of self. In this world of black mirrors we have lost the ability to see ourselves.

This is because we no longer feel as though we have a purpose. However, what many people fail to realize is that we can still discover our purposes as individuals, even though we are slowly becoming directionless as a species. However, discovering individual purpose is a difficult task to undertake as well.

Your third eye is infinitely helpful in this regard. This is because your third eye allows you to look at the world in a completely different manner. It provides you with your spirit guide that can manifest itself in a number of ways. It can be the presence of wisdom within your mind, a sense of direction in your life or even an actual being that you can converse with. Whatever the manifestation, this spirit eye that you awaken with your third eye can help you immensely in discovering your purpose in life.

It allows you to actually see the path that you are meant to follow, and understand what exactly your destiny is. Perhaps more importantly, it allows you understand why you are meant to follow this particular path.

Quit Bad Habits

As a species, human tend to be very myopic in that we only see what is right in front of us. We do not plan beyond the next day, and in many situations we do not look past the next few minutes. This short sightedness is one of the biggest reasons that we have so many bad habits.

Smoking is extremely bad for us, but because it provides us with a few minutes of relaxation we do it anyway. For a few minutes of relaxation a day we shave years off of our life spans. Activating your third eye allows you to examine time in a very different way.

We generally perceive time in a linear fashion. Activating your third eye actually allows you look at time as a circle instead of a straight line. We are able to see our distant future the same way we see our immediate future. If you activate your third eye, you will automatically abandon all of the poisonous habits in your life because you will see that the momentary pleasure that they provide is simply not worth the harmful effects that they have in the long run.

Improve Relationships

This short sightedness that we possess extends to our relationships as well. It has become an all too common story where two people who are perfect for each other, and indeed possess a great deal of love and respect for one another, end their relationship because of a fight. The emotions that were felt during said fight were fleeting, they held absolutely no bearing on the way the relationship would progress in the future, yet because of this petty fight a beautiful relationship has come to an end

There are also several situations where you may feel as though you simply do not know how you can fix your relationship. You may feel insecure about yourself, as though you are not good enough to be in a relationship with your significant other. You might be making the people you love unhappy and don't know how to fix the way you are behaving. There may also be several situations where the people you love may be treating you poorly but you do not wish to leave them because you are used to their presence.

Activating your third eye gives you a much more rounded view of your own life. You are able to see your own flaws as well as how these flaws are affecting those around you. Another important way in which your third eye can help you improve your relationships is that your spirit guide allows you to clearly see who is hurting you and who is a bad influence on you. You can even converse with your spirit guide and seek guidance from them.

All in all, activating your third eye gives you access to a being of unique wisdom. Cosmic awareness makes a lot of things seem petty, and the maturity that follows you connecting with said consciousness can help you to vastly improve your relationships.

Become More Business Savvy

The wisdom that comes from activating your third eye is not just focused on spirituality and mysticism. This wisdom has very practical uses as well. Once you have activated your third eye, you will find that you will have a better eye for business as well. You will just become better at business situations, so if you have always wanted to be an entrepreneur it is a good idea for you to activate your third eye and get an enormous amount of business acumen as a result.

Become More Self Accepting

Everybody feels as though they are worth less than they actually are. Maybe you are awkward in social settings, perhaps you are not as talented as you want to be. However, you are still special in your own way, you possess energy that has specifically come together to form the being that is you.

Activating your third eye allows you to understand this because it shows you that everyone has insecurities. You are able to see people for what they think of themselves apart from what you may think of them, and this will provide you great insight into the way self esteem works. Besides, there are few beings as insightful and as supportive as spirit guides, especially when you are feeling down or have low self esteem!

Achieving Your Goals

There will be several times over the course of your life where you will simply not have any motivation. You will have goals that you want to accomplish, everybody has goals in some form or another, but you would be simply unable to accomplish these goals for a variety of reasons.

You might think that you are not good enough, or that an obstacle you are facing is too difficult to overcome. Activating your third eye expands your mind in such a way that you will be able to come up with solutions to any problems you might face. Achieving your goals becomes infinitely easier after you have activated your third eye, especially since you will now have a spirit guide to ask for advice.

Become More Decisive

In order to become an accomplished individual it is important for you to decisive. However, being decisive is sometimes not as easy as it sounds. Sometimes you will have to make extremely difficult decisions, especially when you are faced with choices where each and every choice you make will end up irrevocably changing your life.

It is in these situations where decisiveness is the best course of action. Making a decision and sticking to it allows you save valuable time and be proactive about solving the problems in your life. Activating your third eye allows you to make decisions more quickly because you will be able to ascertain the outcome of each decision in a more accurate manner. Not having to look at time, as a straight line can be quite useful sometimes!

Become Happier

In our quest for purpose and accomplishment we are often left utterly confused by one very important aspect of our wellbeing: happiness. We look for purpose and we try to accomplish the things we do ostensibly because we feel as though they will make us happy. However, you have probably realized by now that the rat race that is modern life makes you anything but happy.

Activating your third eye does not exactly make you happy. Instead, it makes you content. You become aware of the presence of consciousness far beyond your own and you begin to realize just how petty a lot of the things you are unhappy about are. Contentment is the truest form of happiness, and it is the kind of happiness that you get from activating your third eye.

Heal Your Spiritual Self

We have virtually eliminated the vast majority of illnesses that were once wreaking havoc on the human race thanks to modern medicine. We now live longer, but at the same time we have ignored a very important aspect of our selves: our spirits.

Even though our bodies have become healthy and we are able to live long lives, our spirits remain ill because we are looking for happiness in drugs and mindless entertainment. Activating your third eye allows you to heal your spiritual self as well. As a result, you will live long lives full on contentment rather than the constant struggle to fill the hole within your soul.

Grow Spiritually

As we get more and more connected to each other through technology, we have started to become increasingly disconnected with the concept of our soul. There was once a time where one's soul was the most important part of one's existence, it was a thing that was meant to be constantly nourished and cherished.

Activating your third eye allows you to grow in a spiritual manner. It allows you to look deep within your soul and find the purpose of your existence, thereby allowing you to align the vibration of your soul to the vibration of the universe, which allows you to accomplish the last entry in this list.

Connect With a Higher Power

Once your third eye is activated, your prana will flow through you with ease and you will become aligned with your space in the universe. You will immediately feel a connection with something greater than you.

This entity that you are connected to has many names. Some call it God, others call it a universal consciousness. Whatever you choose to call it, it will make you feel the utter sameness of all life in the universe. You will feel a deep sense of spiritual wellbeing, and will realize that your life is but a small piece of an incredibly mosaic of life that is composed of similarly enlightened beings spread throughout the universe.

Once you are attuned to your spiritual brothers and sisters you are never going to feel alone. One the contrary, you are going to feel their presence and support for the rest of your life.

Chapter 16: Unconventional Ways of Opening the Third Eye

The conventional methods of opening the third eye include yoga, fasting, meditating on the pineal gland and psychotropic drugs. However these are not the only methods that are available to open the third eye. These require good health and must be done in moderation. This chapter throws light on how one can open the third eye through six unconventional methods. Below is a brief overview of how you can do that.

1. Dragon Smoke: One of the unconventional methods through which you can open your third eye is through searching for the dragon smoke. Going from a world to another world mentally is known as searching for the dragon smoke or as the Chinese put it 'riding on dragons'. This came about when Chinese writers and poets made a leap in their written works due to inspiration. This is also attributed towards the long wisps of floating smoke in the center of the art works. This denotes the transfer of the mind from the

conscious parts of the brain to the unconscious parts of the brain. In simple terms, leaping is the charting of territories from known waters to unknown waters and back again. Searching for the dragon's smoke is usually referred to the search for knowledge. This knowledge refers to the enlightenment that one receives upon opening the third eye and therefore blurs the lines between the finite and the infinite. The Chinese refer to this process as learning the knowledge of the Gods because one is riding a dragon and dissolving into the unknown truth about the universe. One can do this by using colors, music and even art. The frequencies of music can lead to new dimensions, viewing the world from a new perspective. The aesthetic sense of sight and the comfort of colors can charter us into a deeper world that is usually hidden away within us. Riding the dragon makes us look deeper, understand deeper and read between the lines. It gives us a sense of clarity. Once we enter this realm, we are able to gather information, search for meaning and understand the truth about ourselves. So it is a good idea to take the plunge and dive deep into your own mind and when you awaken the third eye you would be able to comprehend matters in a more profound manner. This will not only be an interesting experience but an enriching one as well.

2. Unbecoming everything: What this means is that strip all the conflict, confusion and troubles that plague your mind and relax. This will give you a sense of liberation. Enlightenment and liberation is often mistaken to transform you into something but this view is largely flawed. It has more to do with letting go of yourself and channeling your authentic self in a more positive manner. All of us have several layers and these layers are barriers we form which

often makes us lead very complicated lives. By stripping our layers and making ourselves simpler we would find joy in everything. Our multilayered personality has often smothered us and is partially the reason why we are unable to open our third eye. By getting rid of the unnecessary layers that form a protective shield we'd become more vulnerable. It is this vulnerability that can kick open the third eye. Our personality is very similar to that of a Kundalini snake. The Kundalini snake sheds its skin with each chakra. With each layer getting shed, the snake gets stronger and becomes capable of harnessing and channeling the inner energy it possess. With each layer of skin that the Kundalini snake sheds, it is able to regenerate itself and became a better and an enlightened version of itself. We too can adopt this technique and get rid of the unwanted layers and barriers we build around ourselves. This will lead to unburdening ourselves and freeing our minds from petty issues. By shedding each layer over time we'd be able to open our third eye that is often blinded by our social layer, our pretentious facades, and our prejudices among the many others.

3. See the world through a new perspective: We are constantly influenced by our perceptions. These arise out of our experiences and our circumstances. Everything that we view has a hidden meaning or some truth that we are unable to see due to the mind block that comes with our multiple layers and our opinions. By channeling yourself to see the world from an apocalyptic point of view, you will be able to seek enlightenment and become a superior version of yourself. We are constantly focusing on the taught reality, the one that is instilled in us by our parents, mentors and teachers. We take their view and are influenced by their

perspective, which often clouds us from becoming the person that we are meant to be. The caught reality is the landscape we find ourselves in. We often don't choose our experiences and circumstances, these naturally occur to us and this is referred to as the caught reality. The last possibility is the reality that we haven't explored due to our dormant third eye. The reality is the power vested in nature and is naturally present within us. This reality requires channeling and enables us to create a better balance among the realities we face. We are able to perceive better and become more insightful. By viewing the world in its true sense instead of gazing at it from an optimistic point of view or a pessimistic point of view, we'd be able to uncover the truth in everything. This will enable us to open our third eye which will show us the path we seek, allow us to attain clarity and help us focus on substantial things instead of pursuing materialistic things.

4. Practice Counter Weltanschauung dynamics: This principle is derived from the German world Weltanschauung, which translates to worldview. Our views are biased and tilted, this is the major reason we are unable to open the third eye. We are also unaware of our ignorance and blasé about important aspects of the universe. We are so caught up in our worlds with our schedules and priorities that we often lose track of what is important to us. In order to open our third eye we need to practice the art of viewing the world from the opposing views that we hold. This will let us uncover any hidden truth amongst things and also allow us to bridge the gap between what is truly right and what is wrong. We should start this by taking a good hard look at ourselves. We must analyze our situations, our behavior, rethink our perceptions and understand why we hold such

views. This is done through self-examination and self-evaluation. Then, we can start by envisioning ourselves in the opposing view. This will enable us to interpret accurately. This makes us broadminded and widens our horizons. By practicing Counter Weltanschauung dynamics, we are able to develop a holistic view on things. When we develop this, we are able to empathize with things, feel strongly about situations and at the same time we are able to introspect on our true selves. This will kick open our third eye and we will be able to make accurate decisions based on the truth rather than our bias. The opposing view is held for a reason and it is better to contemplate on this rather than just discard it, to truly understand yourself.

5. Practice Faux pas dynamics: Stop over thinking, overestimating, undermining and exaggerating yourself, your circumstances and the people around you. Keep your head cool and be open to new experiences. Realize that adverse situations will not last and neither will excessive happiness. Live in the moment but don't get carried away. With the emphasis laid on material items, we have become increasingly materialistic. We find happiness in things instead of simplicities. Start by not taking things around you so seriously. Let yourself breathe and laugh instead of worry. Start respecting people, understanding them and getting to know them better instead of being focused on only yourself. Do away with selfishness and misconceptions. Be open to new ideas and start living your life the way you want and you will find yourself immensely happier. More importantly, be humble and gracious about people and experiences. Sincerity is the key and you will be able to open your third eye if you let go and experience yourself for the person you are. Spread joy where you go and try to develop a healthy sense of

humor. One that is not crass or offensive. If you stop taking religion, caste and your ambitions so seriously you will be able to express yourself better and be open to new challenges that would reform you. Redeem yourself to become a better version of yourself. Apologize when you can and give people chances. Be forgiving and spiritual instead of religious. Don't let exaggeration; excitement and depression take over your life. Everything in life is transient and once you realize this you will be able to live completely. Laugh at the face of adversity and seriousness. Be transparent and honest. Transform yourself to be a warm person and one who people are comfortable with. This is a sure way you will be able to let go of yourself and stop letting other's opinions influence you. This is a sure fire way to get your third eye to open.

6. Practice Crazy Wisdom: By practicing crazy wisdom, what we mean is find that bridge between maturity and youthfulness. Be able to differentiate between the extremes and find the balance in between and stay on that middle ground. Read and contemplate. Develop your understanding about things and be in peace with yourself. Blur the lines between an amateur and a professional. Be a visionary, have forethought and think about things. Don't dwell on the past or the future but don't be reckless. Most importantly, have conviction. Be wise with your decisions but don't over think things and at the same time be spontaneous enough. Find the middle ground between morality and immorality. Accept your flaws and mend the ones that you think require mending. Stop striving for perfection. Question instead of blinding following anything, be it faith or religion or even an idea. When we start becoming a truer and a more honest version of ourselves, we attain clarity of our identities. This will give us a deeper understanding of ourselves and what we

are truly like in our elements. We get lost in the maze of ourselves and we are unable to find ourselves. We are so entangled with mundane events we fail to experience the vibrancy and the moment of the present and hence we miss out on a lot of opportunities that present themselves before us. When you are in your element you will experience a sort of high that comes with opening the third eye. You will be rewarded with a deeper conviction towards things, a fresh perspective and inner peace. Develop the creative side of you channeling the analytical side of your being.

Chapter 17: Mistakes to Avoid When Trying To Increase Your Intuition

People generally want to feel good and have a smooth transition between the realms. Many complain about difficulty, disorientation and naturally want to feel better. They want to be able to experience the crossing of realms easily and understand their own transition. This experience does not just come about in that manner, it requires effort. What most people don't realize is that it requires an excellent balance. Vibrations and frequencies are the hallmark of every experience; higher vibrations or faster ones come as a result of the range of the frequency. If the experience or transition comes at a high frequency, we might find it a little hard to focus due to the higher vibration. This is what makes it difficult for us to view it with our very own eyes. Increasing your intuition will enable you to sense and see the metaphysical movements that actually take place when you are switching between various realities. When the third eye is open you will be able to sense and understand things more precisely. Similarly you will be able to break down the frequencies and the vibrations that accompany them. In this section, we discuss what the common mistakes are when you trying to heighten your intuition.

1. Giving Up Too Easily

One of the most common mistakes that people commit is that they give up too easily. Opening the third eye requires skill, patience and time. It will not happen overnight and to expect it to happen soon is an unrealistic expectation. Think of it as becoming a great scientist or a dancer. You will not get results in a span of a day or a few days but by constantly practicing you will attain results. Reduce your expectations for in the first go you will not be able to see angles and orbs. Metaphysical energies won't be sensed unless you discover yourself and make it a point to practice it. This is better because if you do happen to see the ghost of people from your life, you will be severely daunted for the rest of your life. Be at peace with yourself and try to remain calm, this will create positive energy vibes. As you meditate you will be able to shift energy and understand its movement. You will take your time to adjust to these frequencies and sense these vibrations. Practice the art of letting go of resentments and negative emotions. Also, enjoy the experience and stop being too focused with just the results.

2. Holding On To Old Habits

We cling hopelessly onto bad habits and negative emotions without letting go of them. These create a block and prevent us from seeing things. Metaphysical beings and energies can only be sensed if you put your effort into emptying your mind. Create a harmonious energy within yourself and be at peace with yourself. These blocks that come up due to bad habits, negative emotions and ill feelings usually cloud our minds and acts as a blindfold to our third eye. These blocks blue and dim our intuition and by removing them we can sharpen our skills a lot better. Let go of toxic relationships, ones that don't make you feel positive and ones that often hurt you. Remove chemical diets and harmful products from your diet. Incorporate healthier options. Get rid of discomfort at home or the workplace. Negative environment has an impact on your mind. Eradicate all potential distracting experiences and people from your life. Take time out to analyze what are the things and circumstances that hinder you and create mental blocks and slowly start by getting rid of them. Also make it a point to get rid of your negative perceptions towards any situation. Be open to learning and reduce conflict within yourself and around people.

3. Taking on Too Much Energy

By taking up energy we imply that when you are empathetic you absorb the energy of the people around you. You start to feel more and you start to pick up other people's feelings subconsciously. When you are with happy people, you feel more happy and relaxed; you pick up their good vibes and good feelings. Similarly, when you are with sad people you feel more depressed, you need a pick me up and you feel let down. When you start to absorb more energy around you, you start to get more exhausted and more involved with other people's affairs. Start by grounding yourself, keep your head to yourself and your feet on the ground and don't get carried away by things. When you start feeling too intensely about something, start channeling those emotions into more constructive things. Kids generally are high on energy and this energy causes them to be hyper. They move far too much, they play a lot more and they laugh more than adults do. Adults require the same amount of movement. When you start channeling your intensity towards movement by jogging, exercising, skipping or playing a sport you start changing your mindset. You feel more relaxed and you start to shed all the extra energy that you have absorbed. When you don't feel grounded you start to distract yourself through unhealthy ways like eating, loading yourself on unhealthy junk, alcohol, cigarettes, gossiping and so on. Be more connected to your physical self. Have a deeper understanding towards yourself and be more focused in yourself over others.

4. Getting Lost in the Realms

Meditating is a beautiful way to attain peace with yourself and let go of resentment. What meditation is not is an escapade. Meditation is no way to escape from situations and problems. Most people who meditate are constantly trying to seek enlightenment through spirituality. They are so focused on this goal that they often get caught up with it and hence do not get results. All metaphysical beings and energies are already present; they just required to be sensed not seen. You need to acknowledge their presence and be aware of them rather than try to befriend them and become one of them. It is very easy to get lost in the metaphysical world and this could have severe implications when done wrong. It could distract you, make you lose focus and play with your mind. You shouldn't try to live the experience but feel and sense it. When you get too engrossed and too caught up in meditation you fail to notice results because you start looking at it as a bargain. You become ambitious towards the goal and you start to treat it like a quest rather than something that one should experience in their lifetime. Focus on finding a balance and seeking out peaceful energy rather than positive or negative energies. Make it a point to enhance your reality.

Chapter 18: Experiences upon Opening Your Third Eye

Opening of the third eye comes with several experiences. You may have pleasant experiences and some that are unusual. Some can even be negative experiences. There are many different ways through which you will know that your third eye is open. In this section, we discuss the possible experiences that you will face when you set your mind into opening the third eye.

You will be able to tell if your third eye is open when you start to experience things differently. For instance, upon awakening your third eye, when you close your eyes you will find intense white dots, colors like blue or purple or even white. You will also be able to see a dark sky with dots or stars. In certain cases you will see an eye shape that is blue or purple in color. In some instances, you might not find the eye shape but a square, a triangle or even a circle that is blue or purple in color.

When you are meditating and focusing on the third eye, you may experience a shifting of activity, a vibration or some sort of pressure buildup in your mind. This denotes that the third eye is in the process of being opened. When you start to experience an out of body experience you will know that your third eye is being opened and soon you can see the world through the third eye.

What to expect after the third eye opening

As stated before when you open or awaken your third eye, you will generally experience some out of the world or unusual experiences. This is more prominent when it comes to vision or sight. You might feel a little exhausted due to pressure exertion. When this happens ensure that you relax and take some rest. When you do open your third eye, you will experience images flashing through your mind. This is more prominent when you are tired. When you start to sleep or relax you get flashes of various images. These images are often disconnected and come from the various dimensions that exist between the various realities. Some of these images can be vivid and clear and would make sense while some others might be blurred or unclear. Whatever it may be your third eye will be able to pick out on these images because your third eye is more focused on energy and can sense vibrations a lot better. The more you practice, the more pronounced your third eye gets and you will be able to make sense of these images. The higher frequencies you experience, the more pronounced your vision gets. This implies that you will be able to transcend across worlds, realms and dimensions easily. Blurred images signify that your metaphysical powers are still weak and still needs work. When your images start to get sharper and take better shape, you know you are developing your third eye.

Higher and Lower Dimensions

When you open your third eye, you also give our vibrations. It is these vibrations that determine the images you see. If you give out low vibrations due to lower frequencies then you will get to see dimensions and realities where souls that aren't put to rest exist. These souls are not souls that have found peace. It implies that you will see people who have been slaughtered, murdered or have committed suicide. These also include people who aren't satisfied after their death due to their lack of fulfillment. These souls are often trapped between realities. They stay between the real world and the alternate dimension and do not find escape. It is better to focus on sending out better vibrations, to see better sights. The minutes you start seeing such sights, it is ideal to give out better vibrations as these sights could scare you. Many people who end up seeing such sights regret opening their third eye due to their fear of seeing dead spirits.

Many people wonder at this stage what to do when they start experiencing such sights. The only advice that can be given is to send out higher vibrations with better frequencies. This will help you attain better sights. Remember than the vibrations you give out determine the sights you see in your third eye. Hence it is best to give out higher vibrations. Be more positive and have a clear mind and you will be able to give out better vibrations. If you are very scared and want to discontinue seeing such sights, ground yourself. Start by distracting yourself in a healthy manner by shedding the extra energy. You can do this by exercising, going for a run or doing an intensive activity that will sap your extra energy. Avoid getting involved in spiritual activities for a while if you feel uncomfortable and talk to people who are present in the present reality. Be cautious when you try to open your third eye and when you make the decision to close it. This is because it will take you a longer time to get your spiritual powers back if you want to get them back. It will take more effort and you will need a lot more endurance to get them back when you close your third eye. If you give out more positive vibrations through higher frequencies you will be able to see better sights. These vibrations include happiness, harmony, love and other positive thoughts. When you give out these energies you will find yourself seeing more developed and pleasing sights. You will be able to see vivid and bright colors, better sights with golden or white hues. In these dimensions, you will also experience peacefulness.

Note that in these dimensions you may also experience a lot of information flow into your mind. These will be a result of shifting of energy that will take place inside of you. The dimensions will shift within you and rapid movement of colors and images can experience this. When you close your eyes you can see various realities shuffling through your eyelids. When these rapid fluctuations of images happen, do not let it hamper you. You might not know how to switch off the sight of your third eye and this might be a scary experience. This is exactly why you should only get into the opening of the third eye when you are very sure and when you are confident in your abilities. Read the information completely before trying anything and then make a decision. When you start to experience movement and lots of images do not get scared. All you will have to do is open your eyes. Try to focus on other things, listen to some pleasing music and do something that is distracting. Have a physical connection with anything, if you own a pet stroke its fur and concentrate on that. If you have a partner, engage yourself in some romantic activity with them. These will turn of the vision of your third eye.

Sensitivity to energies

When you open your third eye you would become more sensitive and susceptible to the energies around you. This includes the positive as well as the negative energy. You would develop a more empathetic attitude towards things as you will develop a deeper understanding of the people around you. When this happens sensitize yourself to pick up the positive vibes that people give over the negative aspects. The positive energy will reflect on your personality and you will be more harmonious. However, you can't completely eliminate negative energy and it is only natural that you absorb some portion of the negative energy or the bad vibes that people give out. For instance, if someone is upset or annoyed with something, then if you are in the same room as them, you will be able to pick up on their emotions. You are likely to be more affected. It is for this reason that spiritual monks and hermits isolate themselves from others. This is because personal contact with people affects them a lot deeper than regular people.

They are able to grasp and hold onto other people's energies and often feel exhausted because of this. With more spiritualized power, the more these types of energies affect you. However, try and focus more on the positive vibes over the negative energies. You can envision yourself in a happier surrounding or imagine golden or white hues. These are all protective methods you can employ to shield yourself from the negative energy when you are with people. Imagine all the energy getting filtered through a large screen of golden or white light. You will find it easier to protect yourself. Another great technique that you can use to reduce the harmful effect of negative energy is to come home and take a shower with some cold water. This cold water will wash away all the impurities both physically and mentally. It will calm you down and help you relax. The water will wash away any of the negative energy that you harbor due to interaction with people. Envision the water physically washing away all your negative vibes.

When you keep practicing this and fine tune your movements, you will find huge relief. The act of washing away the negative vibes in the shower will create peace within you and restore the positive vibes. You will also feel lighter and happier and be inspired to do something. This will come about only after purifying your mind and soul from negative energies that will block you from the path of self-discovery. It is ideal to practice this for a few minutes every day and over time you will start feeling more rejuvenated and fresher after showering. Your energy levels will also start to shift and you will find yourself being more focused on things. You will also develop a more positive attitude and switch to healthy routines. This will improve your health and increase the quality of your life. You will also find yourself more harmonious which will help you attain peace in your relationships, work life and give you a good state of mind.

Other third eye opening experiences

Third eye is denoted with spirituality and hence you can experience strong vibes from opening your third eye. But do not be frightened by the sudden hike in the energy level. You will find yourself more spiritually inclined when you open your third eye. Always remember to be calm and hold yourself together when you open your third eye. This is because opening of the third eye can be exhaustive and an out of the body experience. In the initial stages you may experience light-headedness and you might feel very intensively. However, just let the vibrations take over you. When you give out higher vibrations you will see more positive images. You will find yourself seeing beautiful houses and landscapes that denote serenity and peace. These usually are in gold or white colors and take soft forms. People see still life images and objects as well. They also see creatures who look similar to people and forms which aren't scary. You will get an insight on how the realities are. You will find yourself looking through different dimensions and seeing life in those dimensions. Also note that there are several dimensions. When you get a view of a darkened sky with stars it implies that you are in the fourth level. The trick is to smoothen your transition amongst the various dimensions and not get lost throughout the experience.

How long it takes to experience the third eye opening

First and foremost, do not be impatient with the opening of the third eye. The time taken to open your third eye varies and depends on several factors. In fact, even genes play a role in the opening of the third eye. If you are spiritually advanced or come from a family that makes you pray and meditate you will find yourself opening the third eye a lot easier as compared to someone who is not spiritual. It also depends on the amount of mind blocks you have. If you harbor resentment and ill feelings of jealousy, unhappiness and dissatisfaction then you will find it harder to open your third eye. You can open your third eye in about a week or take a very long to open it. It also depends upon your perception and on various others factors.

Chapter 19: Things You Should Know About Your 'Third Eye'

The first thing you should be aware of is that scientists still don't have a thorough and a complete understanding of the pineal gland. The pineal gland is located in the center of the brain. It is in the shape of a pinecone and is the gland that secretes neurohormone melatonin when we are sleeping. Originally, scientists and researchers believed that this gland was a vestigial gland and was only of use to some primary animals and evolution kept these glands.

Now philosophers, scientists and researchers are constantly working towards the development of the pineal gland. They are trying to find hidden meanings and how it links everything together. By subjecting ourselves to acute sun and bathing ourselves in artificial light, we will be contracting severe illness and diseases including cancers. Long-term exposure to certain chemicals can trigger allergic reactions in the pineal gland. Even working for a long time and not getting adequate sleep at the right time can affect the secretion of the neurohormone melatonin. This can lead to long-term consequences. This can affect our circadian rhythm, which is the connection between our minds, bodies to that of the earth.

The connection between the hours of the day including day and night with us gets affected. Thus by giving our pineal glands a chance to show what they are truly capable of, we not only subject ourselves to a new perspective but also we pave the way to possible danger and disease. Today, research has shown us that there are positive links that have been established between the disruption of the circadian rhythm and heart disease, cancers and diabetes. By tapping into our minds and forcefully affecting our third eye, we can give rise to nightmares and psychological complications that will hinder our performance. The third eye is the home to everything that is scientific and not scientific at all. This is the area where we visit our wildest fantasies, imagination and fandom come from and it for this reason that scientists and mentalists have taken an interest in the gland. The pineal gland is more powerful that we perceive it to be. It can be the one thing that separates us from our light and dark. The more we focus on a side the more we attribute towards it.

The pineal gland holds together several molecules and cells. Some of these only surface during the night time and because of this gland's odd behavior, the extent to which the pineal gland is used is still in question. Scientifically speaking the only information about the pineal gland that is completely understood is the secretion and synthesis of the neurohormone melatonin. This is controlled by our body clock, which is determined by the suprachiasmatic nucleus. The light modulates this gland and hence it is at night that the functions are truly seen. Pineal gland is often referred to as the "principal seat of the soul". This is because it blurs the scientific analysis and the spiritual speculation that surrounds it. Therefore, picking apart the use of the gland is very difficult. In this section we discuss the major facts that you need to know about the third eye.

1. Third Eyes and Theosophistry

Initially, when the pineal gland was first discovered, people assumed that the gland was originally an eye. It was thought of as a regular eye that will be susceptible to light and receives signals through our retinas. There are many speculations surrounding the pineal gland and about how the eye expanded itself onto a brain and that the pineal gland is the home to centralized power. The brain was sued to perceive things using the aid of the two external eyes. The pineal gland or the third eye is the connection between our previous generations and evolutionary states. It holds the spiritual connections that we truly have and aims at rejoining our mind and body along with our spirit and soul.

There are several religious deities that are depicted with three eyes or one eye. Mythical creatures that are found in ancient cultures, traditions and histories influence these. These creatures or beings are said to contain tremendous amount of power, some of them include, Cyclops, Lord Shiva among the many others. There are several references made to this third eye in Hinduism. In Hinduism it is believed that one of the primary chakras, that is, the seventh chakra is Sahasra, which is a lotus that takes the shape of the pinecone like pineal gland. This chakra is attributed towards the unification of spiritual and physical form and the oneness between spirituality and scientific thought. The Greek and the Roman philosophers have always given a superior status to the pineal gland. It was them who ruled the scientific enquiry and philosophical knowledge. Theosophists of the modern era claim that the pineal gland is the doorway or the gateway to the unknown world. It holds within its core secrets that are transpired across the generations. They contain knowledge and wisdom of the spiritual beings and of our past lives. The third eye has developed into the pineal gland. With development in astronomy, our evolution can be studied through this gland. Some animals hold the third eye in its pure form. However evolution has transformed this third eye into the gland in many cases. Animals like the tuatara exhibit photoreceptive third eye, which is called the parietal eyes. History shows that fossils and remains of creatures have a socket in where the pineal gland currently exists.

2. Device Construction for Studying the Pineal Gland

The pineal gland plays an important role in regulating our lives. Our body clock that is determined by the central circadian clock is the one that controls our ability to adhere to time and controls our timing in various situations. It is the one that determines how long we sleep, how long we are tired and so on. It therefore controls our behavior and psychology. It is hard to measure this circadian rhythm and the secret of this cycle is locked away in the pineal glands. These glands are present in both man and animal and in ancient times the scope of the study was limited due to technical complications. Today, with the onset of science and progress in technology, the properties of the neurohormone melatonin can be studied. Professors and scholars from the University of Michigan have formulated a microdialysis which decodes the neurohormone through technology driven, automated computer codes that breaks down the melatonin and analyzes the important compounds of the pineal gland for a certain period of time.

This device generates high-resolution images and pictures that capture the essence of the pineal gland. These images help scientists understand the production of melatonin secreted by the pineal gland and how it affects the body clock. What is currently known is that this hormone is secreted when we are asleep and helps to repair our brain. It also acts as a medium and connects the gravitational forces of the earth and the day and night time zones with that of our bodies. Melatonin is also found naturally in plants, microbes and animals. This hormone is a natural antioxidant. Though scientists are currently exploring the various uses of this compound, it is able to control chronic disorders, autoimmune diseases and helps to combat the degeneration of the body.

The dialysis which was constructed for the study of the pineal gland helps to monitor the secretion of melatonin under different circumstances including jet lag, pollution, heavy pollution, change in the diet, different work environment etc. This helps us understand the way the pineal gland reacts to various conditions and how these conditions affect the functions of melatonin. It also plays a significant role in identifying chronotypes and how certain animals are naturally found to be alert at night (nocturnal creatures) and how some animals are attuned to early mornings. Each chronotype determines the circadian rhythm of the creature.

3. Artificial Light = Dark Future

Studies undertaken by the professors at Harvard University School of Public Health have found that there is a significant link between combating breast cancer and prostrate cancer through melatonin. It is said that the modern sleeping patterns of individuals has come about due to irregularities in diet, gaps in sleeping patterns, excessive technology usage and workload. This has resulted in us becoming unhealthy. This has made us more prone to cancers. The light from artificial lamps and incandescent light affects the pineal glands and have made the risk of developing cancer and other illness more prominent. In fact, the artificial light that has been used to light up the darkness weakens our immune system and long-term exposure cases hormonal cancer.

The team at Harvard published over five research papers each analyzing and concluding the positive links between the circadian rhythm and melatonin disruption that comes about due to light exposure and how it affects the pineal gland. In fact, case studies wherein they used NASA's Defense Meteorological Satellite Program archive and statistics from World Health Organization have shown that women who are more exposed to artificial light especially during the nighttime have seen a significant increase in the development of breast cancer. Further research has also shown that when people move from minimum stipulated exposure to more exposure there is a 36 per cent higher chance of developing cancer and when they exposes themselves for the maximum period their risk chances went up by an added 27 per cent.

The team also used kernel smoothing. This enabled the creation of density maps that showed the correlation between the cancer risk rates and the exposure of artificial light. The research was segregated based on the intensity and height of the light exposure and it was this study that showed a clear link. Algorithms were developed and utilized for worldwide studies that aimed at determining the rate of light exposure in accordance to the weight of the population and how much light each person was exposed to. Using econometric models of regression and correlation they could see the positive link between artificial light exposure at night and cancer rates.

It must be noted that the light exposure varies across terrains. This is because of the lapse in development across countries for instance in underdeveloped countries like Bangladesh or Nepal, the average exposure of light per person is about 0.02 nanowatts for every centimeter squared. However in more technologically advanced countries or even more developed nations in the world the exposure of light is about 57.5 nanowatts for every centimeter squared. Also with progress and evolution we are more exposed to light than our ancestors ever were. About a century ago, human beings attained 12 hours of sunlight each day and were exposed to 12 hours of darkness. This of course is generally speaking, assuming there is no change in latitudes, seasons or any other changes. A couple of decades back after the advent of the light bulb, the days have been extended for a longer period. Also we have some exposure to light even when we are asleep. We have night-lights on or the streetlights that filter through our bedrooms. With more exposure towards LED through televisions, computers and other monitors and devices, we have managed to be susceptible to light exposure. This has managed to break down our immunity that we have attained through genetic evolution and all the development that we have faced since our previous times have gone to waste.

Though we significantly can't do much about the exposure of light in our lives, we can at least try to combat the extent to which we are exposed by making use of natural light to do our work. Use lesser light and going to sleep in a darkened room. Close the blinds and shutters and avoid exposure to light after dark. This is specifically important because the disruption of our circadian rhythm can be carcinogenic.

4. Occult Classic

Pineal glands are more than meets the eye. Though scientifically speaking prolonged exposure to artificial light can hamper and hinder the production of melatonin in your pineal gland, pineal glands have more than just a scientific background from which information is derived. Scientific evidence holds true in most cases however the spiritual speculation that surrounds this mysterious gland is still present. The third eye and the pineal gland are just organs of our mind in accordance to science. Spiritually speaking they are gateways that link our supreme enlightened selves with our current state of mind. They come with an extraordinary past and one that isn't yet explored. They are also said to contain remnants of spiritual powers and supernatural abilities. The mysteries that surround the third eye are a constant source of fascination with writers, spiritualists and occultists who are trying to develop and prod into the third eye.

In fact, several movies and books talk about the supremacy of the pineal gland. Writers, playwrights and dramatists often create characters with a range of supreme powers all associated with the third eye.

In movies like In From Beyond, crazy and eccentric scientists turn into zombies who eat brains through the activation of their pineal glands. In other movies like She Devil, the leading female character turns into a monster. Her pineal gland gets activated and she ends up becoming a savage devil. In many cases, the third eye is also given a sexualized nature that is used to seduce people and control them through manipulation. It is because of these theories that have very little scientific evidence that sexual dysfunction medical supplements contain melatonins. Though, the extent of the use of the third gland is unexplored and shown in different lights in the entertainment industry, scientists believe that there might be some correlation between the two.

Many TV shows and serials have depicted the pineal gland as a source of power. It is said to be a gland that can manipulate and control various aspects of the world. With lack of scientific understanding people have allowed their imagination get the better of them. In many cases, the pineal gland is said to be the powerhouse of psychic ability and of mental communication. It is influential and its spiritual magic is tapped into through fiction. The pineal gland is more developed that we think it is and due to the tiny amount of information with regards to the abilities of the pineal gland writers and storytellers have spun tales about its usage.

Chapter 20: How To Tell If You Are Having A Spiritual Or A Psychic Awakening

There are several ways through which you can tell if you are spiritually awakened or if you have attained psychic enlightenment. In this section we discuss the various ways through you can tell if you have attained spiritual awakening. Given below are the top few ways to know for sure.

Tingling Sensation or Pressure

The easiest way through which you can find out if you have attained enlightenment is by feeling some sort of pressure or a tingling sensation. The third eye area is present between your eyebrows. This is where the chakra is present. When you feel a tingling sensation in this area you can be assured that your third eye is awakened. The tingling or the pressure happens due to two major reasons. One is that you are able to detect and absorb energy and vibrations from your surroundings. Two, you are more focused on your chakra and your inner spiritual energy is flowing and developing. During the initial stages of practicing meditation, the pressure or the tingling sensation can be very strong.

Connection with Spirit

Another common way through which you know if you are having a psychic awakening is by feeling a stronger connection towards spiritual things. You can feel and sense vibrations of spirits and you are more sensitive to the energies of the people. Spirits are all around us and celestial beings and ghosts are present in our surroundings and we are not able to detect their presence. When you sense the presence of people, angels, your guides, beloved people who have passed away, you know that you have a psychic connection. You can also detect the presence of other people's spirits.

Desire to be Away from Negativity

Negativity saps your energy and when you have a spiritual awakening you can feel the energy of the people or your surroundings a lot more strongly. This in turn can make you pick on the negative vibrations given by people. You become more empathetic and attuned to the feelings and emotions of other people. At this stage, your sensitivity is heightened and you absorb positive as well as negative energies easily. Negative energy can exhaust you and therefore you might find yourself shying away from circumstances and people who bring out negativity. You also try to become less conflicted and avoid arguments.

Desire to Eat Healthier Foods

You start becoming more conscious of your body. Remember, your body is a medium and you exist in this world in the vessel that is your body and therefore it is your obligation to protect and harness your body in the healthiest manner. When you receive awakening, you start to eat a lot more healthy foods. This is because when you are awakened your intuition is heightened and you give our vibrations at a much higher wavelength and frequency. Natural foods, which are unprocessed like fruits and vegetables, have a higher frequency and this allows you to harness and channel your inner spiritual energy. You feel bogged down by eating heavy food especially junk food.

Desire to Learn and Be More Spiritual

In many cases, you start to seek knowledge. You spend your time doing constructive activity like reading and learning. You start to shed your old ways and break your bad habits and focus more on enriching yourself through knowledge. You are also able to grasp onto concepts more easily and you find yourself understanding things with more precision and accuracy. You also become more spiritual. You contemplate often, you also introspect. You are also constantly looking for inspiration and feel a deeper sense of purpose. You start to take part in the path to self-discovery and spend your time learning as much as possible.

Frequent or Vivid Dreams

You also start to experience vivid dreams and you remember these dreams. The amount of dreams that you see when you are asleep depends upon how awakened or enlightened you are. Dreaming frequently is one of the common signs of psychic awakening. This is because you are not resisting what your mind is creating. Your body is at rest and your mind is actively creating and harnessing energy and channeling this spiritual energy into various forms. In this state you are also able to move across dimensions and you are also able to switch from the different state of minds. You will now be able to gather information from the subconscious parts of your mind in an easier manner.

Heightened Sensitivity of Your Physical Senses

This implies that your physical senses manifests and you are more aware of your physical sights and sounds. For instance, if you are able to hear a lot better you will be able to see movement through your peripheral vision or you might be able to see golden or white hues of light or dots. These imply that your senses have heightened and they are getting stronger. You also can see clearly and you become more observant. You also become receptive to minor details and minor sounds. Even your taste buds become more superior and you can taste the food you eat and pick the flavors apart.

Intuitive "Hits"

When you are awakened your intuition becomes more superior. Your gut feeling becomes more pronounced and you are able to sense things easily. You also have intuitive hits where you feel that something may happen. This might be both exciting as well as frightening. Note, that you might not see premonitions; however, you might be able to foretell how something goes. You are able to sense the outcome of things. You can also control your psychic ability; you can shut your third eye and open it when you want to. You can also practice intuitive guidance to familiarize yourself with your strong intuition.

Headaches

You are also more susceptible to headaches and migraines. These are common and though they can be a pain, the channeling of energy causes them. When you are spiritually awakened your mind starts to shift the energy inside. It also absorbs more energy and vibrations from the surroundings; this can cause an overload and cause headaches. If your headaches are getting progressively worse then you can start by soaking your feet in some warm water. This helps to shift your energy from your head to your feet. You can also add essential aromatic oils and bath salts to the tub of water. This will help you relax. However take note to check if it is not something more serious. Headaches can also imply physical problems and eyesight issues. So go to a doctor or a medical practitioner and get it checked.

Losing Friends - Making New Ones

One of the few unconventional ways through which you know you have psychic awakening is when you start to lose out on some of your old friends. This is because you start to become more mature and more heightened. You stay with only people who give you positive vibrations and you stop paying attention to drama or gossip. You outgrow your old friends and feel a sense of disconnection with some of them. This is because you start to view the world differently and you feel detachment with materialistic bonds and a sense of aloofness towards unnecessary relationships. Things which were previously important will stop being important and you will find yourself treading towards enlightenment.

Looking younger

When you embark on the path of spiritual awakening, you will find yourself looking a lot younger. This is because you will have multiple out of body experience. You will start feeling a deeper sense of purpose and what previously affected you will have no impact on you. You will start to remove emotional issues from your life. You will avoid problems and you will become a more resolute person. All the previous judgments and misconceptions that you had will vanish and you will find yourself becoming more calm and relaxed. You start to enjoy yourself a lot more and you become content. When this happens you start to look younger.

Feeling of Oneness

When you feel spiritual awakened or attain psychic enlightenment, you will become more content with yourself. You feel strongly for people and you connect with people easily. You also have a deep connection towards animals and plants. You are able to understand the emotions of animals a lot better and you might even find yourself in the company of animals. You will feel completely at home with yourself and exude only positive and harmonious vibes. You start to feel united towards things and you are flooded with transcendent awareness. You might also feel unconditional love towards things. You will not harbor ill feelings or negative emotions. You will find yourself enjoying solitude and a sense of detachment as well as attachment towards people and circumstances.

Chapter 21: Mediums and Intuition

The most important thing you should know is that all of have some amount of intuition within us. This intuition depends upon a variety of factors. Every single one of us is intuitive at some form or manner. Intuition is believed to be the gut feeling or something that has been hidden in our soul and our subconscious. It is believed to be a strange mysterious wisdom that surfaces during certain times. Research and studies have shown that most people are born with an intuitive sense and everyone has the sixth sense. This sixth sense is not often paid attention to because studying it is quite difficult.

The sixth sense is more pronounced in some people while it is blurred or dull in some others. Everyone is not a medium however everyone does have the power to become mediums. Think of it as someone who has the talent to learn something like playing an instrument, everyone can play an instrument, but not everyone can play it exceptionally well. Similarly, mediums are of two categories. They can be born or they can be developed. A person who has the natural ability to perceive the sixth sense are called naturally born mediums and those who develop and fine tune their sixth sense as they progress are called latent mediums.

Latent mediums are those who have a higher sensitivity towards the sixth sense. They have a slightly higher intuition level as opposed to regular beings but their intuition intensity is a lot lesser as opposed to naturally born mediums. They have a form of natural inclination towards intuition and this is why some people have a good gut feeling. While it might not be so apparent, the skill can be developed over the course of time. This requires some amount of natural skill. Development of your sixth sense requires time and arduous effort. This requires an inner transformation and spiritual awakening that only comes about after long hours of meditation and contemplation.

Now the question arises how exactly can one person tap into their sixth sense? How can one person tell how good their intuition is and how can they identify themselves as a medium? The answer to all this might seem like just mere meditation, however unlocking your psychic powers and intuition has so much more to do with just mere meditation. Meditation is just a small part of the exercise. There are many processes you will need to undertake for you to be able to refine your sixth sense. This does not just imply contemplation, meditation and challenging your core beliefs. Even your outlook and the company you keep might require changing if you ever want to truly develop your sixth sense.

In this section of the book we look into what you truly require to fine tune your intuition. How to develop your sixth sense and what are some processes you can easily follow to get it developed. This chapter also throws light on how to identify yourself as a medium. Intuition is inner wisdom and in order to develop this inner wisdom, you would require patience.

Some of the easiest ways through which you can tell if you are a medium is if you have experienced the following:

1. As a child did you ever have a fear for the dark because you feel something lurking in the shadows?

2. Did you ever feel like you never managed to fit in and you felt disconnected to people?

3. Did you explore spirituality and metaphysics and develop a fascination for supernatural beings and energies from a young age?

4. Do you sometimes see beings or spirits? This could take the form of light sources or energies or even spheres that float in air.

5. Were you more sensitive towards energy and could you detect emotions and feelings of people?

1. Your Consciousness needs to be purified

One of the first steps you need to do when you want to increase the power of your intuition is to clear and purify your consciousness. This implies getting rid of all the things that hold you back. You can only develop a good intuition if you clarify and purify your mind. When you hold a lot of negative aura within you, it is going to block your third eye. This can result in your intuition to become weaker. Resentments, ill feelings and personal troubles should be let go of. You should be able to let go of the past and forgive yourself for the mistakes you have committed.

Channel all your negative emotions into something constructive. You can choose to write down your feelings to reduce the intensity of them. Try your best to get rid of feelings of remorse, regret, anger, jealousy and unhappiness. Make a conscious effort to detoxify yourself from these. Make room for more positive feelings and good thoughts. Cultivate feelings of happiness, peace and harmony. Forgive all the people who have wronged you and practice kindness and humility. Have a positive attitude and look at the bright side of the things. These are often easier said than done but make an effort to be a better person.

Sit down and take a moment to recollect all your thoughts. Think deeply of all the people who have wronged you and who you have wronged. Envision all the bad facets of your life, the terrible experience and the negative circumstances that you have found yourself in. If you are surrounded by negative people and people who are constantly holding you down, then get rid of them. Surround yourself with positive people. These include people who support you and cheer you on. These should be people who are compassionate and uplift you to higher grounds. Practice compassion and put yourself in a good position.

Also start to acknowledge karma and know that bad karma is going to affect you. Be your natural self and get onto the road of redemption. Stop complicating yourself so much and give yourself a good analysis and get rid of all those qualities that are holding you back.

This also means you must start acknowledging and working through your bad karma while also fulfilling your dharma perfectly. Most importantly, start practicing acceptance and look at life from a new perspective. Be confident in your abilities and be at peace with who you are, where you are and have faith in where you are going to go.

The reason behind stripping yourself of negative qualities is to make yourself a good vessel. The secrets of the universe are only going to infiltrate you if you keep your mind pure. If you are blocking the third eye with negative perspective and misconceptions, then you will find yourself having a very poor intuitive. The secrets and the hidden truth are going to bounce right off due to ego, pride and negativity. You will also be channeling and giving our negative vibrations that can attract angry spirits and negative experiences. Ensure that you have the deepest connection to yourself in order to connect with positive spirits. This might take a long time, but by practicing and understanding yourself you will be able to become a better and a refined version of yourself.

2. Get a Spiritual Mentor or a Guru to Help You

If you truly want to develop your intuition then it is a good idea to get a spiritual guru or someone who can help you develop your intuition. It is a good idea to find a spiritual person and the effort will pay off eventually. This is because you will get better wisdom and insights when you have someone who will guide you. Most spiritual gurus would have gone through what you went through and will be able to help you in your journey. You can get tips and points from them to cultivate your intuition. They would have undergone a similar experience and hence they will be able to channel your thoughts a lot better.

One of the most prominent points to note when looking for a spiritual guru or a teacher is to find someone who does not charge an exorbitant rate. If the person you have narrowed down to charges a high fee or demands for materialistic things then you would have gone to the wrong place. A guru needs to be someone who is inwardly as well as outwardly spiritual. He or she must not lay emphasis on material gains and must be more interested to take you as their disciple and reform you over scamming you off your money. Basically they should have a good value system.

The second aspect to consider when looking for a teacher is someone who has attained spiritual awakening. You might find a lot of people who are treading the path you are currently walking however these aren't helpful. Find someone who has been spiritually awakened and someone who has developed their intuition. The person you choose as your teacher or guru must be one who has attained the powers that you are looking to achieve. If they haven't then it will be difficult for them to guide you and you will be stuck in the middle ground and unable to access your true potential.

Also look for someone humble. When searching for a teacher the person must reflect the qualities that you are trying to attain. They should be at peace with themselves and should be able to channel your energy well. They should also exude positive thoughts, harmony and serenity and must not have negative thoughts and ill feelings. They should be collected and calm. Be aware of several fake teachers out there. There are many people who would claim that they would help you but really won't. The guru or teacher must be enlightened and humble. They should not be patronizing nor should they be haphazard.

Be wary of all the people who claim to be gurus. Watch out for people who are pretentious and those who are trying to scam you or rob you. Do not get into unnecessary conversation with people who come across as pretentious. They usually end up being false teachers who would just be in it for the money and your attempt would have been futile. True spiritual teachers are not robbers and there a certain positive force that you will be able to feel when you are with them. While they all will charge a fee, true spiritual gurus do not focus only on the monetary or materialistic gains. They will give you advice and points without charging much. You can also read their books and attend any workshops or training if they offer any. These usually come at a price but are proven to be quite effective. You can also understand the techniques when you go to them.

Most importantly, avoid going to people who are going to make you spend your money for everything including the things they are doing. Your guru should be one you feel comfortable with and not feel apprehensive about. If your teacher is making you do strange things or things you are not comfortable with. They shouldn't scare you or alarm you by saying things such as you are cursed or that you will never attain spiritual enlightenment and so on. Be sure to have a spiritual teacher who lets you make your decisions and understands what you want. You shouldn't report to anybody who makes you feel inferior nor should be at the company of people who are going to dictate decisions for you. They should impart wisdom and knowledge and let you traverse through your own path.

When looking for a teacher be patient and take your time with the effort. You can't find good teachers over night but you can always search for one. In the meantime try to develop yourself and understand what you want. Cultivate qualities like humility, positive attitude and be sure to redeem yourself. Be a blessing to your teacher when you do happen to find one. The path of spiritual enlightenment is yours and only yours to walk. Develop the qualities of a good student and be open to learning. When you develop upon your characteristics you will find yourself in an easier position to gain awakening. Be sure to support your guru and you will win their devotion and support as well. This will make them want to help you and share their knowledge and wisdom with you.

3. Start to Cultivate and Enhance Your Vision

By cultivating your vision, we imply that you look both forward and backward to see the past, present and future. Be able to understand your past and analyze the experience. This also means that you should try and understand the past of others. Develop an empathetic attitude. This will help you understand the path a person has taken, their choices, their decisions, how these impacted them. Understand that everyone has had different experiences both in their current and past life. Develop a deeper sense of understand towards yourself and towards other people and you would be able to see the past.

Start by developing your memory. When you have a powerful memory and are able to recollect details. This will help you see the past. You need to be able to know what you did a few hours ago. If you do happen to visit a psychic, they are likely to be able to tell what you have done in the past life and what kind of a person you are. When they tell you such things it is a good rule of thumb to put them to test and ask them what you did a few hours ago. If the psychic is incapable of telling what you did a few hours ago then be assured that they are incapable of telling what you did in your past life. Intuitive people are able to tell what kind of a person you were in your past life but the trick isn't to be able to just feel the past of the people but to be able to visualize the past. You must have much more than just an idea of how the past of the people looks like.

Seeing the present is a lot easier and yet a lot deeper than you might think. It implies that you should be able to understand the technicalities of the present or the current time. This includes the ability to understand the bigger picture. You should be able to identify with people's karma and their actions. You should also be able to tell how the forces of nature interact with people and how it impacts people. In order to understand the present be able to visualize it you need to be organized and have a clear and a crisp mind. You shouldn't be scatter brained and you should adhere to a good schedule.

You should also develop the ability to look into the future. Clearing our mind and purifying your conscious can do this. Develop your memory and have a good schedule. Have healthy habits and shed falsities and pretentiousness and you will be able to see the future.

4. Fine Tune Your Healing Abilities

Develop your ability to heal people. This is done through a variety of ways. You need to become a genuine person at the forefront. Start by wishing nothing but happiness upon people. Wish them well and be honest to them. Start to visualize the energy of the person especially the Prana energy. Under stand every connection in the body. The Prana energy when weak can affect the body. Understand the mechanics of this connection and make use of it to heal the physical form. Practice Reiki to channel healing chakras and harness positive healing aura through your body. This will help you heal others and create a spiritual barrier that makes you stronger.

5. Sharpen and Cleanse Your Five Senses

In order to develop your sixth sense you will need to sharpen your other five senses. Make yourself more sensitive to all the senses. Stay away from negative substances and those that could harm your other five senses. Clean and purify your five senses and take care of them. Watch only positive things, read positive things and write and preach positive things. Eat healthy and good food and avoid eating junk. This way you will be able to slowly but surely cleanse and sharpen your five senses.

6. Follow a Schedule and Maintain a Regime

Start by having a good healthy outlook in life. If you want to develop spiritual awakening and sharpen your intuition you can only do so if you make the required changes in your life. Be disciplined and practice what you preach. Sleep at a stipulated time everyday and wake up at the same time everyday. Eat healthy food and commit yourself into practicing everyday. Wake up and meditate for a while everyday. If you want to awaken your third eye you need to be focused and that should be your end goal. If you are lazy and uncommitted you will not attain liberation.

If you follow a good schedule, one that is not too hectic and one that allows you to breathe, you will be able to find yourself in a better position. Practice meditation regularly and you will be able to see a difference. If you follow a schedule you see results faster. A daily regime will also enable you to connect tasks and follow things. When you clear your mind and tune your body towards a particular aspect your spiritual awakening will start to respond. When you have a disciplined lifestyle, everything else will fall into place. The energy that you spend on tasks will be significantly reduced and this energy will be used to harness your psychic abilities. This will also allow you to harness the energy and forces of the sun and moon. If you wake up before the sun rises you will be able to absorb the energy of the sun and you will find yourself being more rejuvenated. The sun and the moon are important aspects when it comes to affecting our psychic abilities. This is due to the circadian rhythm that connects the universe with our physical and mental state.

BONUS CHAPTER - Three Secret Tips for Opening Your Third Eye

As a bonus, here is a section on the three secret, mostly unknown tips that can help a person to open their third eye. Practice these especially when you find yourself in a situation where you need to meditate quickly for any reason whatsoever.

Follow these steps exactly how they are and you will see immediate and great results.

Relax:

Imagine yourself floating on water. You are light and relaxed. Your body is weightless. The first thing that you want to do when opening your third eye is to relax your body, mind, and emotions. This may sound overly intuitive, but when you enter into real relaxation, you'll discover how tense you are in your daily life.

One of the best visualizations that I've found extremely effective for getting into a completely relaxed state is to imagine that there is a brilliant, white cloud floating above my head. This cloud is my friend as it rests atop my crown and starts to absorb all my worries. I've never known how much stress my body can store before the cloud leeches it all out of my body. It leeches the pain and stress out of my whole body. My eyelids feel like someone has removed wires from beneath them. My ears feel light. My fingers are slightly pulsing due to the relief I am experiencing. Even my heartbeat is getting slower and I am finally settling into the mattress. Try and sink into a comfortable prone spot here for best results.

Continue visualizing this cloud like a gentle vacuum down your body. Let the tension be sapped from your shoulders until they are light. Let the weights fall off from your spine as your body sinks into and becomes one with the comfortable mattress. Continue doing this until you reach your very toes and feel the bad heat get leeched from your body leaving you feeling cool and comfortable.

Focus On Your Forehead:

Don't doze off! You might want to go to sleep at this point because this will be the most relaxed you have felt in years and while that is a good idea, remember that you are doing this for your third eye. Hence, close your eyes and focus your energy on your focus.

Relax and don't think about how silly this is. Focus and think about the center of your forehead. Remember to keep thinking about that spot. Try and visualize your third eye opening.

Just bring your attention to the center of your forehead. Become aware of your skin, bones, and muscle in the center of your forehead.

After only a few seconds of focusing your attention on the center of your forehead, you'll also notice something that has nothing at all to do with your physical body.

You'll notice a definite pressure in the center of your forehead.

Open Your Third Eye:

The longer you focus on your third eye, the more intense your experience will be. Be warned at this stage since you are unleashing great and raw power. In a few moments, you might feel like your head will want to explode from the sheer power of the whole ordeal.

As you exhale, rather than just letting air out of your lungs, let out a long sigh.

This sigh will be similar to the sign of the 'Eem' we discussed above. This sigh is also called a Bija Mantra. This is the sound of sustenance, creation and destruction as well. This sigh will help you open your third eye as well. This is the point where you will feel like a doorway has opened in the middle of your forehead. This is your third eye opening. This is when you will start feeling the powers of intuition almost attacking at you with great intensity. Use these powers to draw scenarios, as you would like them to happen in your life? The reason? You are one with the earth. You are setting things in motion.

Focus on these situations and start sending energy into them one by one. You will start feeling a raw energy flowing through every cell of your body. This means that you are creating waves on the surface of the earth. You will pretty soon witness your scenarios becoming a truth and happening as you willed them to initially.

Conclusion

Now that you have come to the end of this book, I would first like to express gratitude for choosing it and investing time in reading it. Third Eye awakening is a wonderful experience that unlocks mystical powers within you. The process needs time and should not be rushed. It is recommended that you engage an experienced trainer who will help you nurture this skillfully. Once fully developed, your Third Eye will lead you on a path where your spirituality will connect your life to nature and everything else around you. Everything around you will be in sync with your energy, and your life will be full.

All the material in this book was gathered from various sources, which have in depth study on the subject of the third eye. As you gain better understanding on the topic, you have better chances of awakening your own third eye.

By now you already have an idea of the immense potential of how the third eye can affect your life. In order to see these changes, you need to make a constant effort for a long period of time. The changes come soon after you have started stimulating your third eye. They may be subtle at first but the effects are obvious in the long run.

As you practice meditating with your third eye in focus for a longer time, you reach a higher state of consciousness. You gain better understanding about the universe and your inner self as well. It will help you in forging a connection with the greater powers and seeking their guidance. As you become more receptive and sensitive to other forces, your psychic powers are also honed. You can see into greater dimensions and even see the possibilities of the future. All this will help you in leading a much more fulfilling life with purpose.

If you find the guidance in this book helpful, you can even recommend it to others who feel can benefit from it. The world will be a much more different place if people everywhere started letting go of un-important things and looked at life with the third eye instead.

RECOMMENDED READING

TANTRIC SEX: Couples Guide: Communication, Sex And Healing

hyperurl.co/tantric

Auras: Clairvoyance & Psychic Development: Energy Fields & Reading People

hyperurl.co/auras

NLP Subconscious Mind Power: Change Your Mind Change Your Life

hyperurl.co/NLP

MIND READING: Clairvoyance and Psychic Development

hyperurl.co/mindreading